Savannah

A Gracious City of Enterprise

Copperfield Publications, Inc.

Enjoy the view overlooking the Savannah River, and watch the ships from all over the world pass by. Photo curtesy SCVB.

Published by COPPERFIELD PUBLICATIONS, INC.
2880 West Oakland Park Boulevard, Suite 220
Fort Lauderdale, Florida 33311

Produced in cooperation with:
Greater Savannah Chamber of Commerce
Savannah Economic Development Authority
Savannah Area Convention & Visitors Bureau

Art direction, design and production by Christine Spencer-Bates
Editor: Cheryl Badeaux
Assistant Editor: Christina Wood
Contributing writers:
Christina Wood
Betty Darby
Melanie Simón
Richard Wittish
Allison Hersch

Front cover design by Christine Spencer-Bates

Library of Congress Control Number: 2006935210
ISBN: 0 9647106-7-6
Printed in USA
Photo this page SCVB.

Table of Contents

Each December, the Downtown Neighborhood Association hosts a popular Holiday Home Tour, which raises money for historic preservation. Photo curtesy SCVB.

Acknowledgements

No project of this magnitude is completed in isolation. The Publisher extends a generous word of appreciation to: the contributing authors whose depth and insight into the fabric of the community was a major factor in this production; photographers whose images are spectacular. Also acknowledged are the individuals and their organizations who volunteered their time and insight toward the completion of this production. Among these are: The Honorable Otis S. Johnson, Ph. D. Mayor, the City of Savannah, Melissa Yao, Savannah Area Convention and Visitors Bureau, St. Andrews School, Gulfstream Aerospace Corporation, JCB, Savannah/Hilton Head Airport, Skidaway Institute of Oceanography, Savannah State University, St. Joseph's/Candler Hospital, Memorial Health, Armstrong Atlantic University, Savannah Technical College, Benedictine Military School, Westin Hotel, Savannah Sand Gnats, The Mulberry Inn, Hampton Inn, Juliette Gordon Low Birthplace, Savannah Candy Kitchen, The Shrimp Factory, JT Turner Construction, SCAD and Brooks Stillwell.

Special thanks to everyone in the business community who rallied behind this worthy cause and whose wisdom and understanding of this project was a cornerstone in its production. My strongest words of appreciation are reserved for Brynn Grant, Rick Winger, and SEDA, William Hubbard, Margaret Mary Russell, and Savannah Area Chamber. Without their enthusiasm, cooperation, direction and immediate comprehension of the significance of this endeavor, this book may have never reached first base. There are many people who deserve a great deal of gratitude. If we have overlooked anyone, we apologize: it was not intentional.

Fort Pulaski, named for polish born, Casimir Pulaski. Pulaski became a true military talent for fighting in battles across Europe. He was mortally wounded in an attempt to retake Savannah from the British and died on the American ship, WASP. Photo curtesy SCVB.

Old Fort Jackson. is the oldest standing fort in Georgia.. Named after Lt. Col. James Jackson. (Jackson was born in Devon, England.) The fort was built to defend the city of Savannah against naval attack. During the war of 1812 the fort was armed with 24 pounder canon. The fort was never attacked. Photo curtesy SCVB..

Introduction

Office of the Mayor Savannah, Georgia

Otis S. Johnson, Mayor

Greetings,

It is my pleasure to welcome you to the beautiful City of Savannah. This publication is the perfect tool for you to learn what makes Savannah, Georgia so attractive to businesses, families and tourists.

When General James Edward Oglethorpe and the 114 travelers of the good ship "Anne" landed on a bluff high along the Savannah River in February 1733, Oglethorpe named the thirteenth and final American colony Georgia, after England's King George II. Savannah became its first city.

Located along the Georgia coast, residents enjoy a high quality of life, thanks to award-winning schools, abundant natural resources, a thriving economy, and a vibrant business community. We here in City government are guided by our vision of making Savannah a safe, environmentally healthy, and economically thriving community for all of its citizens.

Our residents enjoy being able to work, live and play all in one of the country's most beautiful cities. More than 6.9 million visitors a year find Savannah rich in beauty and history while preserving tradition and heritage. Our lovely parks and squares, our unique restored historic district and the incomparable natural beauty of our islands and beaches are all complimented by our warm, southern hospitality.

Companies continue to locate and grow here in Savannah, thanks to our business-friendly environment and community partnerships. On behalf of the Savannah City Council, I congratulate the Savannah Chamber of Commerce on 200 years of service to our community. The Chamber is an essential investment for the future of every business and your commitment to making business better has been and will be appreciated for the centuries to come.

Employers represent a diverse array of business types, from manufacturing to military to technology and tourism. Superior institutions of higher education as well as advanced healthcare options combined with Savannah's laid back way of life add to the uniqueness of this diversified community.

We hope you take the time to discover Savannah's charms, natural beauty, architecture, and rich history while you are visiting because you are our guest and Savannah loves sharing her treasures with you.

Sincerely,

Otis S. Johnson, Ph. D.
Mayor

The Mighty 8th Air Force Heritage Museum, where one can experience
an unforgettable journey of sound and sight. Photo courtesy SCVB.

Ships of the Sea Museum was founded in 1996. Its exhibits of model ships, antiques and paintings represent the Great Era of Atlantic trade between England & America during the 18th and 19th century.
Photo curtesy SCVB.

CHAPTER ONE

History of Savannah

By Richard Wittish

From its beginning, Savannah has been a city rife with the entrepreneurial spirit.

In fact, the spot where Savannah developed was a place of enterprise even before the city's birth.

Upon landing in the new colony of Georgia in 1733, the Englishmen who founded Savannah were greeted by Indians who had moved to the area less than 10 years before, and by the owners of a trading post established in 1730.

Since then, Savannah has grown to be a seaport, a destination for tourists, the home of manufacturing plants, a base for the military, a center of higher education, a drawing card for artists and historic preservationists and filmmakers, and, most recently, a hotbed of wireless and computer technology.

Playing major roles in the city's growth have been the Savannah Area Chamber of Commerce and the Savannah Economic Development Authority.

But in the winter of 1733, way before any of the aforementioned came into being, the site where the city developed was a wilderness.

One of Oglethorpe's first acts after founding the colony was to lay out a city, which he named Savannah.

His city plan called for the creation of a series of squares to be bordered by homes and public buildings.

He laid out six squares; 18 more were added later. Photo courtesy of the Georgia Historical Society.

The 128 Englishmen who came to that new world in February 1733 were intent on making their new home a place of commerce. Unlike many from Europe who had settled in colonies north of Georgia, the first citizens of Savannah were not driven primarily by a desire for religious freedom; instead, they were seeking new beginnings that were economic in nature.

The settlers were recruited by James Edward Oglethorpe, an English soldier, statesman and philanthropist. While serving in Parliament, Oglethorpe became an advocate for prison reform, and his involvement in that led him on a quest to find work for his unemployed countrymen.

Together with a colleague, Oglethorpe determined that North America might hold the best promise for honest, hardworking Englishmen who were down on their luck and in need of new starts in life.

The two men petitioned King George II for a grant to land in America on which the "worthy poor" could make a living, and the king on June 9, 1732, approved a charter giving Oglethorpe and 20 associates what they wanted. The group was incorporated as the "Trustees for establishing the Colony of Georgia in America."

The charter was a shrewd move by the English crown, for the new colony would serve as a buffer between the Spanish in Florida and rapidly developing South Carolina. It was also hoped that Georgia would provide natural resources for English industry and a market for English exports.

Oglethorpe was the only trustee to make the initial trip to Georgia - a voyage aboard a 200-ton ship named the Ann, and he and the settlers were welcomed to the New World by 100 or so Indians - the members of the Yamacraw tribe of the Lower Creek nation. The tribesmen were led by Tomochichi, an 80-year-old chief who, apparently seeking greener pastures, had in 1725 brought them from western lands to the coast. Also on hand was Mary Musgrove, a half-Indian, half-white woman, who with her white husband John had established a trading post near the Indians' village. She played an important role in the early days of the colony by serving as an interpreter between the Indians and the English, who formed an alliance that aided the settlers in securing their new home.

One of Oglethorpe's first acts after founding the colony was to lay out a city, which he named Savannah. His city plan called for the creation of a series of squares to be bordered by homes and public buildings. He laid out six squares; 18 more would be added as Savannah grew and prospered, and they gave the city a uniqueness and beauty that serves as the linchpin of Savannah's tourism industry - today a key segment of the town's diversified economy.

Throughout Georgia's early development, Oglethorpe continued to serve as its protector and benefactor. When he left the colony for the last time in July 1743, the town of Savannah had 353 houses, and stores and warehouses had been built. Also, the threat of invasion from Florida had been quelled, with Oglethorpe two years earlier leading his soldiers to victory in a battle over a much larger Spanish contingent on St. Simons Island to the south of Savannah.

James Oglethorpe was the seventh of nine children in a large, wealthy English family. Enrolled at Oxford, he received a commission as ensign at the age of 16 and became a member of Parliament at the age of 26. Upon his arrival in Georgia the colony of Savannah was formed into the vision of the leader. Oglethorpe would act as doctor and judge to the families that joined him on the venture, and many texts refer to him as a "strict disciplinarian." Oglethorpe's design of Savannah's physical layout was an elaborate plan that consisted of a series of wards built around central squares, with trust lots on the east and west sides of the squares for public buildings and churches, and tithing lots for the colonists' private homes on the north and south sites of the squares. Photo courtesy of the Georgia Historical Society.

Erected in 1910, the magnificent bronze Oglethorpe statue by Daniel Chester French was the last of the great monuments placed in the squares on Bull Street. James Oglethorpe continues to watch over his city from his high loft in Chippewa Square. The square was laid out in 1813 to pay tribute to the victory of American bravery at the Battle of Chippewa during the War of 1812. Photo courtesy of the Georgia Historical Society.

In 1752, the first phase of the development of Savannah and Georgia came to a close when the trustees resigned their charter and the colony became a royal province.

Under the crown, Savannah sputtered for a time, then flourished under the guidance of the colony's third royal governor, James Wright, who arrived in town in 1760.

That same year, the city's first wharf was built, presaging Savannah's role as a great seaport. A total of 3,400 pounds of rice was exported in 1760, with that commodity and indigo and silk being the most lucrative crops during the colony's early years. Yes, silk, which the English thought could be produced because of Georgia's climate. And, for a time, the imported silkworms and mulberry trees that sustained them did their work, as silk became an important export. But the silk industry died out in the 1760s as other crops became more profitable.

Under Wright, the colony grew in terms of population and production, and the great plantations of the coastal plain began to be developed. In November 1766, the governor reported to an acquaintance that the number of white colonists had increased from 6,000 to about 10,000 since his arrival and that black population had gone from 3,578 to 7,800.

Exports of rice in 1765, Wright said, amounted to 10,235 pounds - triple the output from 1760, and, he stated, "in 1761, we loaded only 42 sail of sea vessels, and the last year we loaded 153, and on an average of much greater burden."

While things were looking up economically in Savannah in the mid-1760s, many residents of the American colonies began to express dissatisfaction with what they felt was unfair taxation by the English government. Those feelings of resentment festered during the ensuing decade, and calls for rebellion and independence were the result.

In Savannah, a group of dissidents called the Liberty Boys met, convened provincial congresses in defiance of Wright, and celebrated the onset of the American Revolution by stealing powder from the city munitions room and shipping it to compatriots in Boston for their struggle against the British. On January 18, 1776, with English warships off the Georgia coast, officials of the provincial government placed Wright under house arrest, ending British rule in Georgia until late in 1778, when Redcoat troops landed, routed the colonial defenders of Savannah and sacked the city, returning Wright to control in the process.

Savannah was a key to the Revolutionary War in the South, and an attempt at retaking it from the British was made in the fall of 1779 by an allied force comprised of American, French, Haitian and Irish troops. They began a siege of the city in the latter part of September that culminated in the Battle of Savannah on Oct. 9. The fight was focused on an allied attempt to breach the British defenses at an earthwork fortification southwest of the city. The struggle for that strong point - the Springhill Redoubt - ended in a bloody defeat for the attackers, and Savannah remained in British hands until near the end of the war. Americans finally regained control of the city in July 1782.

In the period between the end of the Revolutionary War in 1783 and the beginning of the American Civil War in 1861, cotton became king in the South, and Savannah benefited greatly.

Exports of cotton went from 1,000 bales in 1790 to 90,000 bales a year in 1820, and export revenues zoomed from less than $500,000 in 1794 to $14 million in 1819, when Savannah had grown to be the sixteenth-largest city in the country. Eighteen-nineteen was also the year in which a group of local businessmen made history by backing the voyage of the SS Savannah, the first steam-powered ship to cross and re-cross the Atlantic Ocean.

Sir James Wright (1716-1785) was an American lawyer and jurist and the last British Royal Governor of Georgia. He became the third appointed Governor of Georgia in 1760 and was arguably the most popular Royal Governor of the colony. He successfully negotiated with the Indians and the Crown to open new lands to development. He retired to England in 1782 and died in London. Photo courtesy of the Georgia Historical Society.

CELEBRATING
200 YEARS
1806-2006
SAVANNAH
CHAMBER

The year before saw the arrival of English architect William Jay, whose designs gave the city numerous structural masterpieces, many of which are still standing today. Jay's work and that of other noted designers and builders filled the city with beautiful homes and public edifices as residents made use of the wealth they had accumulated.

It was also during this period that a chamber of commerce came into being. Merchants and traders of the city met on Dec. 13, 1806, at the City Exchange and appointed a committee of seven to draft a constitution for the government of that chamber. The committee reported back to the city's businessmen on Dec. 30, proposing 17 rules that included provisions calling for initial membership fees of five dollars; for membership to be open "only to merchants, traders, factors and insurance brokers"; and for fines for "officers refusing to serve after being elected." The rules were unanimously agreed to by the 85 "subscribers" in attendance.

According to sources at the Georgia Historical Society, that first chamber was organized on January 6, 1807, when its officers were elected. Historical Society correspondence also expresses a belief - based on researching of the city's newspapers - that the chamber went out of business in 1827, when it "must have ceased to operate . . . and a new Savannah Chamber of Commerce was organized in 1841."

The chamber's mission since that time was summed up nicely in a tract published in 1932 stating that the organization "is used to promote industry, commerce, education and the highest aims of society."

"The work of the Chamber of Commerce," the document declared, "involves the development of industry, merchandise and business generally; the promotion of civic welfare in education and society; and the bringing about of any condition which makes Savannah a better place in which to live and work."

Savannah flourished during the early to mid-1800s, with a high point occurring in 1843 when a railroad called the Central of Georgia was completed, linking Savannah in the east to Macon in the west. A few years later, a connection from Macon to Atlanta was made.

The city's high times came to an end in the 1860s, when Georgia and other Southern states clashed with the North over slavery and states rights. Savannah, as a major seaport of the fledgling Confederate States of America, found itself blockaded for much of the civil war that started after the Southern states' secession from the Union. In one of the few instances of fighting that occurred in the area, the blockade was inaugurated after Federal troops bombarded and captured Fort Pulaski, a large brick structure guarding the Savannah River near its entry to the ocean.

In December 1864, as the fate of the Confederacy was being sealed, Savannah became the goal of Federal troops headed east from Atlanta in General William T. Sherman's March to the Sea.

The city was defended by a decisively outnumbered contingent of Confederate soldiers, and they wisely slipped out of town, avoiding capture but leaving Savannah to be taken by the North on the 21st. That Christmas Eve, President Abraham Lincoln received a welcome holiday gift - "the City of Savannah," as Sherman put it in a telegram to his leader, "with 150 heavy guns and plenty of ammunition and also about 25,000 bales of cotton."

Throughout Georgia's early development, Oglethorpe continued to serve as its protector and benefactor. When he left the colony for the last time in July 1743, the town of Savannah had 353 houses, and stores and warehouses had been built. Photo courtesy of the Georgia Historical Society.

The Green-Meldrim House, the Parish house of St. John's Church, was General William Sherman's headquarters during his march to the sea.
From this house Sherman sent President Abraham Lincoln a telegram giving him a holiday gift - "the City of Savannah," as Sherman put it to his leader, "
with 150 heavy guns and plenty of ammunition and also about 25,000 bales of cotton." Photo courtesy SCVB.

In one of the few instances of fighting that occurred in the area, a blockade was inaugurated after Federal troops bombarded and captured
Fort Pulaski, a large brick structure guarding the Savannah River near its entry to the ocean. Photo courtesy SCVB.

Thus was Savannah spared the fate of several Southern cities that were razed by Union troops, and, within a year of the end of the war in 1865, the city was back on its feet. In 1868, Savannah was exporting in excess of $50 million in material and goods - much of it cotton.

The last 30 years of the 19th century was a period of progress and prosperity. Savannah's first electric light was turned on in 1883; the city's first artesian well was sunk in 1885; a railroad to nearby Tybee Island was completed in 1887, paving the way for creation of a seaside resort; and the town's first brewery opened in 1889. Black residents - freed from slavery and on their own for the first time - built institutions, formed business associations and developed their own culture.

The Savannah Cotton Exchange was organized in 1872, and the Savannah Naval Stores Exchange was formed a decade hence, with the latter becoming the Savannah Board of Trade a year later. The establishment of those bodies was evidence of the continuing importance of cotton to the economy and the growing significance of forest products industries.

The Griffin is the symbol of authority for the Cotton Exchange. Photo SCVB.

In mid-March of 1891, the city's receipts of cotton reached more than a million bales, which was more than 100,000 bales beyond the record of any previous year-long period. Cotton receipts for the last fiscal year of the century were more than 1.1 million bales, with shipments close to that number. During that time frame, some 310,000 casks of turpentine and more than 1.1 million barrels of rosin were exported from Savannah, as were more than 146 million board feet of lumber. A total of 157 building permits were issued, representing $750,000 in improvements.

Savannah's growth continued in the early decades of the next century, with residents erecting a new city hall, creating the town's first residential subdivision - Ardsley Park - after the end of World War I, and building an airport that was opened in 1929.

Another significant development was the establishment in the mid-20s of the Savannah Port Authority, which would evolve into the Savannah Economic Development Authority. The Port Authority was created by legislative act in August 1925 after being overwhelmingly approved by the state's voters the preceding November. As an outgrowth of a movement to establish a state port in Savannah, the authority was given broad powers that included regulating the traffic of the harbor; maintaining and building public wharves and warehouses; and maintaining the depth of the water at those wharves.

The Port Authority was also given the right to issue bonds and to acquire land for the development of terminal facilities.

Eventually, the authority would, in addition to being a "watchdog" over the functioning of the port, assume the responsibility of conducting a program of industrial development for Savannah and the surrounding area.

By 1950, the authority could take credit for increasing the depth of the Savannah River shipping channel from 20 feet to 34; playing a principal role in developing the port under the program overseen by the Georgia Ports Authority, which had been created in 1945; locating a Union Bag and Paper Company plant, then the largest integrated kraft mill in the world, on the Savannah River; and developing a tract for use by the Southeastern Shipbuilding Corporation, which produced nearly 100 Liberty ships during World War II.

The latter two accomplishments were particularly important because they occurred during an era when Savannah was suffering through a decline in cotton growing and through, along with the rest of the nation, the tribulations of the Great Depression. Union Bag brought much-needed jobs to Savannah in the 1930s, and the shipbuilding endeavor employed some 15,000 workers.

The Cotton Exchange, established in Savannah in 1872, did not get a permanent home until 1886. The building on Bay Street, known to Savannah residents at the time as "King Cotton's Palace," was designed to stand out from its neighboring buildings as a symbol of cotton's importance to the city's economy. For nearly a century, trading in the Cotton Exchange on Savannah's waterfront set world cotton prices. Cotton farming was greatly expanded following Eli Whitney's invention of the cotton gin, an event that took place near Savannah in 1793. Shortly thereafter, cotton shipments from the area soared to more than two million bales annually. Photos courtesy of SCVB.

Also contributing to the local economy during the Second World War was the fact that the city became a staging area for bomber aircraft and crews headed for action in Europe and the Mediterranean. The city's airport was converted into an air base and continues to serve the military today as Hunter Army Airfield; another military field created west of Savannah during the war became the site of what is now Savannah-Hilton Head International Airport.

The city's Chamber of Commerce apparently was undeterred by the war, for its annual report for 1942 showed the organization busily recruiting volunteers for a civilian defense council; operating a service to care for thousands of civilian war workers who had "thronged the city"; and promoting Savannah by distributing 36,000 pieces of "carefully planned folder advertising."

Ten years later, the chamber took a significant step in its development by renovating and moving into the Cotton Exchange building on the riverfront. The chamber was a bit ahead of the times, for in the mid-1950s, Savannah's historic preservation movement was born when a group of seven prominent women banded together to rescue an architecturally important downtown house from demolition. Their effort led to the establishment of the Historic Savannah Foundation, which from 1955 through 2005 saved 350 buildings, in the process keeping the downtown a viable place in which to live and greatly enhancing Savannah's ability to attract visitors.

Responding to the city's promise as a destination for tourists, the chamber created a Visitors and Convention Bureau in 1962, and, 13 years later, opened the Savannah Visitors Center in a former railroad terminal on West Broad Street (now Martin Luther King Jr. Boulevard). The center serves as a hub of information and transportation for tourists, some 6 million of whom visited the city in 2004.

Once housed at the Visitors Center, the chamber now has offices in a renovated bank building on Bay Street, from which it serves some 2,000 members, acts as a catalyst for workforce development and strives for the retention of area military bases.

During the last half of the 20th century, Savannah grew to the south and east as new subdivisions were created, and the city built a new airport and revitalized its riverfront and downtown shopping districts. The historic preservation effort took off and was abetted by the development of the Savannah College of Art and Design, which has restored more than 50 buildings since its birth in 1979. The city gained international recognition as the venue for the yachting events of the 1996 Summer Olympic Games.

Tourism boomed - in part because of Savannah's role as the setting for the best-selling book, "Midnight in the Garden of Good and Evil" - with several hotels being built to accommodate the influx of visitors.

Early in the 21st century, Savannah was expanding to the west and developing as a center of high-tech business, with that effort being spearheaded by the Savannah Economic Development Authority, which in March 1989 had assumed that name after 64 years as the Savannah Port Authority.

Frank Leslie's Illustrated Newspaper

Scene in the Principal Square of Savannah, Georgia, on arrival of the news of the occupation of Tybee Island, south of the Savannah River.
Photo courtesy of the Georgia Historical Society.

SCENE IN THE PRINCIPAL SQUARE OF SAVANNAH, GEORGIA, ON ARRIVAL OF THE NEWS OF THE OCCUPATION OF TYBEE ISLAND,

E. K. Gordon & W. W. Gordon standing in the front of a handsome carriage.
Photo courtesy Juliette Gordon Low Birthplace.

Juliette Gordon Low (center of photograph) gave the girls of America and the world career opportunities,
outdoor activities and the fun they so desperately wanted. Photo courtesy Juliette Gordon Low Birthplace.

Join the list of special visitors - American Presidents like President Taft in 1909, First Ladies, Generals and movie stars who were graciously entertained by Daisy, (Juliette Gordon Low was nicknamed Daisy) Nelly & W.W. Gordon in their elegant Oglethorpe Avenue home. Photo courtesy Juliette Gordon Low Birthplace.

CHAPTER TWO

Business, Finance & Trade

By Betty Darby

Savannah first built her fortune on the gifts Nature gave her - a friendly climate, rich soil, plentiful trees and a broad, slow river that opened the city's front doors to the world. As the city closes in on her tricentennial (mark your calendars: it's in 2033), some of those gifts continue to pay off while new sources of riches have been developed.

Agriculture as an economic force is essentially gone from Savannah and Chatham County. But the shipping trade that once carried the region's cotton to world markets has flourished from those beginnings. Vast acres of pine trees fueled the development of the pulp and paper industry, and other manufacturers followed in those footsteps. Now, as many believe manufacturing has passed its prime in this country, Savannah continues to add new manufacturers and is stepping up to claim its share of developing knowledge-based industries.

More than a century ago "Cotton was King." At the turn of this century Savannah is more ideally situated, more diverse, and is keeping a vigilant eye on the future by strategically aligning the community's resources with those required by creative and technical businesses. Photo courtesy SCVB.

When studying what makes Savannah tick financially, it's logical to start where the colony's founder started - the Savannah River. This winding waterway is the unifying thread that runs through the city's past, present and future.

Savannah's first docks were along River Street at the foot of the bluff on which the city stands. Here, bales of slave-grown cotton, barrels of naval stores, and other agricultural products were shipped out to the world, and manufactured goods were brought in. Warehouses lined the riverfront to house the goods, and the streets leading up to the city level were paved with cobblestones that had traveled as ballast in sailing ships.

Ships still ply the Savannah River, and in numbers and size that would have amazed the first merchants shipping out of Savannah's port. The docks themselves, however, have moved upriver - almost out of sight, but seldom out of mind for those with an interest in Savannah's economy.

To understand the success story of the Port of Savannah, it is necessary to understand the evolution of cargo shipping in the last 30 to 40 years. Before, that evolution depended on changes in the ships themselves, with those powered by sail giving way to those powered by steam and then those powered by internal combustion. The latest round of changes, however, had nothing to do with how the vessels got from port to port and everything to do with how the cargo was packaged.

Goods are now packed in containers of identical size, which are then stacked as high and as wide as possible across the decks of massive ships designed expressly to handle these stacks. At the destination port, a crane lifts the container from the ship and can place it directly on the chassis of a tractor-trailer rig or a railroad car. Expenses and turnaround time for cargo are slashed dramatically by the new system.

But only after significant capital investment could ports benefit from the new way of moving cargo. The container ships required massive cranes to reach across their bulk. Because these ships were so much bigger than the generation which preceded them, they required deeper navigational channels and higher bridges. If ample rail access and efficient truck gates weren't in place, the speed advantage that containerized cargo gained in unloading would be lost to riverside bottlenecks.

The Georgia Ports Authority, the governing body for the Port of Savannah and the state's other port facilities, saw the changes that containerized shipping would herald, and prepared for them with major construction projects. The payoff? Today, the Port of Savannah is the fifth busiest container port in the country. More than 18 million tons of cargo were shipped through the port in the fiscal year ending in June 2005.

Having room to expand has been part of the success story for the Port of Savannah. Many American ports became encircled by the cities they served, with urban land values and uses choking off the possibility of expanding economically. But because Savannah's ports of today are upriver from the city, located in an area of mixed industry and open land, expansion has been possible. A new container berth completed in early 2006 gave the port 9,800 linear feet of berthing space.

The direction of the shipping industry in the last few decades seems to defy geography. Because of well-developed freight rail lines, as well as access to Interstate Highways 95 and 16, the Port of Savannah is today a direct competitor with ports on the Gulf Coast and even on the West Coast. The determining factor in that competition is the speed with which cargo can be taken from the ocean to the nation's hinterland.

Containerized cargo has spurred development of another subset of the shipping business - the distribution center. Major national retailers that import vast quantities of goods (especially from Asia) find it convenient to marshal that merchandise at a central location and reallocate it for dispersal to stores throughout the region. Such distribution centers are considered economic development plums because they require construction of massive, high-tech, high volume warehouses, and because they create jobs. A healthy supply of distribution centers is also helpful for ports competing for additional service from shipping lines, since the customers of those shipping lines have built facilities nearby.

The Home Depot led the development of distribution centers in and near Savannah. At least 10 more such centers have followed, the most recent being Target. While the Port of Savannah is clearly predominantly a container port, it also handles cargo in other ways. The Georgia Ports Authority has two major terminals in Savannah - the Garden City Terminal, which specializes in containers, and Ocean Terminal, which handles a smaller volume of traditional breakbulk cargo and other materials. The smaller terminal even handles some vehicle import/exports, although the vast majority of that business is left to the state's other deep water port in Brunswick, which has developed specialized facilities needed for large scale vehicle trade.

Also, while the Georgia Ports Authority is the largest player in the field by far, private industries along the Savannah River also have their own dedicated docks handling everything from ore to oil.

While the Georgia Ports Authority is the largest player in their field by far, private industries along the Savannah River also have their own dedicated docks handling everything from ore to oil. Photo courtesy SCVB.

Savannah is more than a gateway for goods to move in, out and around the country, however. We make things here - from big, shiny expensive things to chemicals that are ingredients that do everything from make a sports car's metallic paint shiny or the logo on a candy shell legible and edible. And the city's manufacturing history includes accounts of corporate knights in shining armor riding to the rescue and how elbow grease and entrepreneurship turned a mechanic into a millionaire.

The knight-in-shining-armor story might sound like an exaggeration - unless you were around for the Great Depression. The year was 1935 and Savannah, like the rest of the nation, was trapped in that economic disaster. Then, a New Jersey-based paper mill came calling. Fresh water, cheap land and lots of pine trees were the draw for the Union Bag Corporation. It built a plant that went on to become, for many years, the largest employer in Savannah.

Now, whether Savannah was ever really a company town for Union Bag (later Union Camp) is debatable, but there's no denying the paper plant was a major political influence and a major provider of charitable largess. More importantly, Baby Boomers throughout Savannah and Chatham County grew up on groceries bought with Union Camp paychecks.

Corporate fortunes of the paper industry worldwide have changed, with stricter environmental regulations and the globalization of paper production. Union Camp itself was acquired by the larger International Paper in late 1998, by which time it had already contracted from its peak size. Although International Paper today is a major player in Savannah's manufacturing community, it is no longer the dominant influence in that sector. Technology and regulation have drastically reduced the famous "smell of money" that was once a paper plant's signature scent. More tangible traces can be found in the middle class lifestyle "the Bag's" payroll financed for the last two-thirds of the 20th Century in Savannah.

The mechanic-to-millionaire story takes us away from paper and into the air with Gulfstream Aerospace Corporation. An ambitious man with a yen for flying would take a small aircraft plant in Savannah and build it into a worldwide leader in the construction of corporate jets known for their speed and range.

Allen E. Paulson was the aviation entrepreneur, and his life story is the improbable-but-true tale of a 30-cent-an-hour aircraft mechanic who would live to see the company he founded sell for $5.3 billion. He had a talent for refining the design of aircraft parts, and he parlayed that talent into the purchase of an aircraft plant that became Gulfstream Aerospace. Over the course of his career, he would be involved in the company's ownership twice as it changed corporate hands in the merger-and-acquisition-happy 1990s.

Paulson is dead now, but the company lives on in good health. It is now a division of major defense contractor General Dynamics. It produces jets for the tycoons of industry, celebrities-turned-pilots (as well as celebrities content to be passengers), and Middle Eastern royalty. Its customers also include the U.S. military and the armed forces of other nations.

Gulfstream is headquartered in Savannah, although it has smaller plants scattered across the country. From its sprawling and well-secured plant alongside the Savannah/Hilton Head International Airport, it launches both finished products and "greenies," or structurally complete but unfinished aircraft destined for finishing touches at other facilities.

Savannah based Gulfstream Aerospace Corporation produces jets for the tycoons of industry, celebrities-turned-pilots (as well as celebrities content to be passengers), and Middle Eastern royalty. Its customers also include the U.S. military and the armed forces of other nations. Photo courtesy Gulfstream Aerospace Corporation.

An ambitious man with a yen for flying would take a small aircraft plant in Savannah and build it into a worldwide leader in the construction of corporate jets known for their speed and range. Allen E. Paulson was the aviation entrepreneur, and his life story is the improbable-but-true tale of a 30-cent-an-hour aircraft mechanic who would live to see the company he founded sell for $5.3 billion. Photo courtesy Gulfstream Aerospace.

Joseph Cyril Bamford launched the construction and agricultural equipment manufacturing company that bears his initials, in 1945. He began his business in a garage that measured 12 feet by 15 feet.

Today, JCB's world headquarters is one of the finest engineering factories in Europe. The company that began as a 'one man band' now employs over 6,000 people and produces over 250 products – with its North American headquarters in Savannah, Ga. Photos courtesy JCB.

As the major manufacturing facility in Chatham County, Gulfstream provides lots of production careers. But it also provides something of perhaps equal importance in the local economy - a voracious appetite for engineering talent and a drive to see that the educational resources to support that appetite are available locally.

These are just two examples of the industries at work in Savannah and Chatham County. There are plenty of others, from Kerr-McGee and its titanium dioxide plant to Byrd Cookie Company's boxed benne wafers to Brasseler USA's dental drills. But more informative, perhaps, than a mere listing of what rolls or pours off local assembly lines is the evidence of continued growth and innovation in the manufacturing sector.

By and large, economists will tell you that we must look to the knowledge-based industry or the service sector to replace manufacturing jobs lost to global competition. But the Savannah area can point to recent success in the industrial recruitment field - not to mention a large, tasty megasite all set up for the next big prospect to come along.

Think back to the late 1990s. The economy was booming. And the largest heavy construction equipment manufacturer in Europe - British-based J.C. Bamford - was looking for a home for a North American assembly plant for its backhoes. At stake was the construction of a massive, high-tech plant and several hundred jobs, with the potential for growth. Fierce but secretive competition went on for months.

Savannah's combatants in the struggle were the Savannah Economic Development Authority (SEDA), which is the local economic development organization, and the Savannah Area Chamber of Commerce, backed up with the state's own economic developers.

Weapons in such competitions are things like labor statistics, demographics, climate, transportation systems, tax structure, and other hard, cold, objective factors. But there are more subjective factors that come into play as well, everything from the quality of local restaurants to the ease of getting in and out of the local airport. Savannah's advocates pulled out all the stops and, in addition to the more serious presentations, their tactics included having a key recruiter meet a Bamford delegation at the airport while driving a backhoe and arranging for an elementary school chorus to sing "God Save the Queen" at one evening's pre-dinner ceremony.

You can see the results of the recruiters' efforts today as you drive between Savannah and the Savannah/Hilton Head International Airport. JCB (as the Bamford firm is known in this country) has its new production facility up and running and, as befits its status as the company's North American headquarters, several shiny yellow backhoes are positioned to be seen to advantage from Interstate 95.

Air service at the area's Major Airport, Savannah / Hilton Head International, is provided by AirTran Airways, American Eagle, Continental Express, Delta, Delta Connection, Northwest Airlink, US Airways and United Express. The bustling airport plays a major role in Savannah's economy. Photo courtesy Savannah/Hilton Head International .

Among SkIO's resources is the 92' R/V Savannah, which carries a crew of four and up to 14 researchers. It is equipped with a wet and a dry lab, and works in both the ocean and rivers. Photo courtesy Skidaway Institute of Oceanography.

Savannah has long been researching its own future. The city is home to several research-oriented institutions whose work has major implications for the region.

For example, there's the Herty Foundation. This organization is named in honor of Dr. Charles Herty, the scientist who unlocked the chemical secrets that made southern pine a cash crop. It was founded in 1938 and for the early years of its existence focused on work that would benefit the pulp and paper industry.

Today, the Herty Foundation is an independent contractual research and development organization, working in confidence with a variety of industries to perform lab and pilot scale development of products. The new focus is on advanced materials.

Another research player is the Skidaway Institute of Oceanography, a unit of the University System of Georgia. Here, scientists tackle a broad range of topics using the ocean, local beaches and marshes, estuaries and tidal creeks as their open-air labs. Among SkIO's resources is the 92' R/V Savannah, which carries a crew of four and up to 14 researchers. It is equipped with a wet and a dry lab, and works in both the ocean and rivers.

The Savannah campus of Georgia Tech, in addition to providing area students the opportunity to earn a prestigious engineering degree without relocating, also provides economic services. It is the force behind the Advance Technology Development Center, which helps entrepreneurs launch and grow successful technology businesses.

It's one of those ever-shifting terms: today, knowledge-based businesses; yesterday, high-tech; tomorrow, who knows? While the term keeps shifting, the concept at least is clear - we're talking about an elite business sector that is using or, better yet, creating technology to do new and different things faster and better. Cities everywhere want these companies because they're high paying, low impact and prestigious, staffed with creative people who can live and work anywhere they choose. Savannah is no exception.

With an eye toward increasing Savannah's share of knowledge-based businesses, the Savannah Economic Development Authority is fostering an effort known as The Creative Coast. Now, both Savannah and Chatham County governments are chipping in.

To date, The Creative Coast counts more than 300 "brain-based" businesses in Savannah (see, we warned you the terminology keeps shifting.)

Joining forces on the same mission is the Coastal Business Education & Technology Association, better known as C-BETA. This organization provides networking and educational opportunities for the technology community, as well as sponsoring scholarships and recruiting venture capitalists.

Savannah can already point to more than one major success story in this business sector. Local entrepreneurs began just over 10 years ago to develop software for cellular telephone billing. They've since sold the enterprise to VeriSign, creating a couple of local fortunes in the process.

It's impossible to review the Savannah area's economy without saluting the military. Hunter Army Air Field started its life as an Air Force Strategic Air Command base during the Cold War. At the time, it was on the edge of town; today, it's firmly embedded in the middle of the city.

About 6,000 military personnel are based at Hunter, and there are another 24,000 soldiers in nearby Hinesville at Fort Stewart, the base of which Hunter is considered a part. Among the Hunter population are Ranger and special operations aviation units.

When you consider Coast Guard units that patrol the Savannah River and coastline, an Air National Guard unit that flies C-130s, and the Marine Corps Recruit Depot at Parris Island nearby in South Carolina, you see why the military estimates its regional economic impact at $3 billion.

On a lighter note, Savannah has hopes of reestablishing what was once a thriving little industry of serving as a movie location. Between 1975 and 2000, Savannah was home to some 40 movie or television productions. Forrest Gump's bench was here, and Glory's troops marched off to the Civil War through our streets.

But better tax climates lured filmmakers elsewhere, and a major motion picture hasn't been made in Savannah since 1999's Legend of Bagger Vance. In 2005, the Georgia General Assembly rewrote the tax incentive package, and perhaps the glitter of Tinseltown will once again be peaking through our Spanish moss.

Savannah salutes the military: which provides an estimated regional economic impact of $3 billion. Photo courtesy Savannah State University.

1. Rendition of the new SEDA building on Hutchinson Island. Photo courtesy SEDA. (Savannah Economical Development Association.)

2. Johnson Square the first square to be laid out by James Oglethorpe in 1733, down town business center. Photo courtesy the City of Savannah.

3. Financial Institute, Chatham Bank built by J.T. Turner Construction. Photo courtesy J.T. Turner.

4. The City Hall location of the city's government, built in 1905. Photo the City of Savannah.

5. The ship industry plays a major role in Savannah's economy. Photo courtesy the City of Savannah.

6. The Trade Center built on Hutchinson Island, across the river from the famous River Street, with 20,000 sq. ft. of space. Photo courtesy SCVB.

. Back drop photo of Wright Square built in honor of James Wright the last and popular Royal Governor of Georgia. Photo courtesy The City of Savannah.

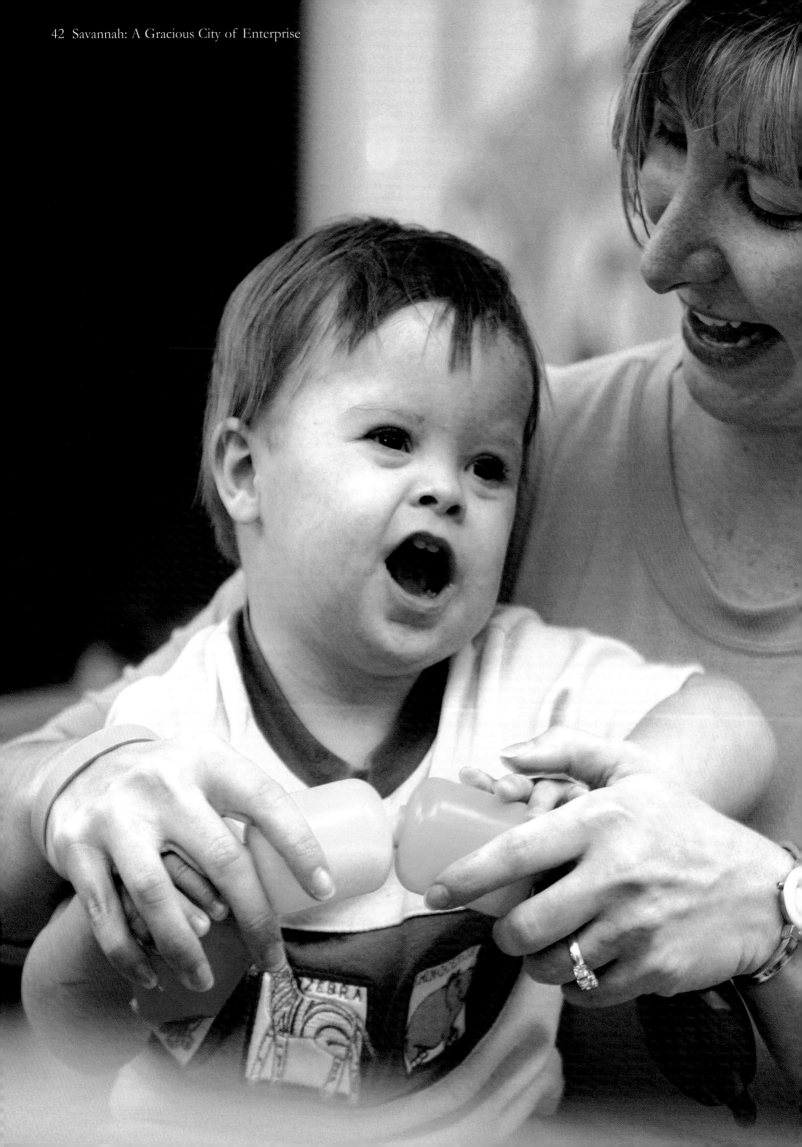

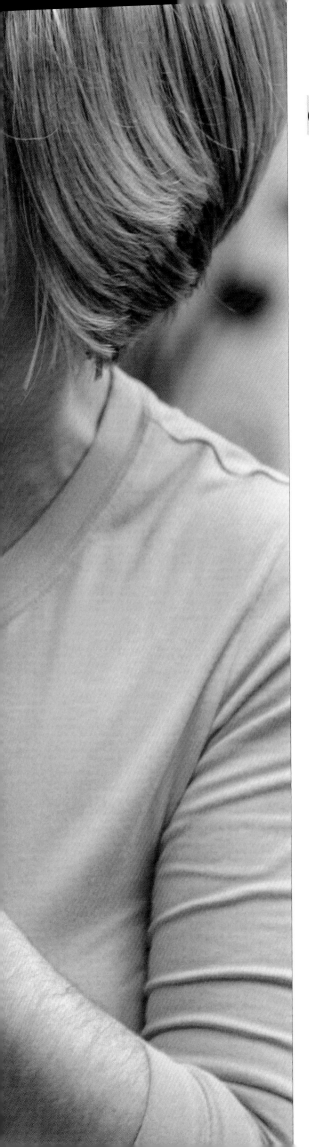

CHAPTER   THREE

Health Care

By Melanie Simón

T he role of healthcare in Savannah, not unlike the rest of the nation, is expanding and redefining itself on a continuous basis. In the face of increasing healthcare costs and new attitudes towards overall wellness, Savannah's medical community is responding to the task, quickly and efficiently. As this coastal city evolves into an ethnically diverse community, local healthcare providers are responding to each group and its own unique healthcare risks and cultural differences. As well, Savannah's hospitals also prepare as the Baby Boomer generation reaches retirement age, many of them making the decision to settle in the South.

As costs increase in healthcare, Savannah's medical caregivers are taking an active role in addressing the immediate concerns of patients. New services are now offered advising patients on medical management in regards to claims, benefits, planning consultations and chronic disease management, which plagues more than 100 million Americans in all areas of obesity, diabetes, congestive heart failure and depression.

Optimum health care is available for patients of all ages and sizes. Savannah boasts an abundance

of quality facilities and health care services for its many residents.

Photo courtesy Memorial Health.

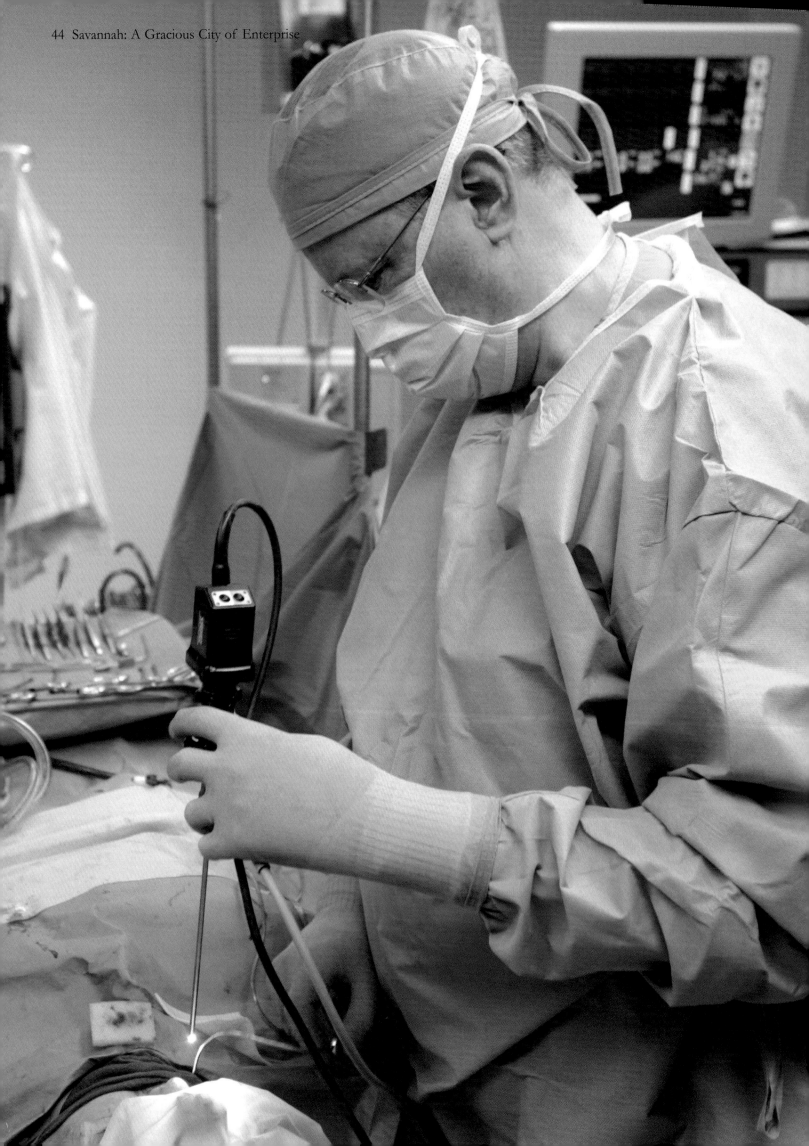

Savannah is equipped with some of the most technological-savvy healthcare facilities in the country. Memorial Health University Medical Center is the regional territory medical center, meaning it provides counties in southeast Georgia and southern South Carolina with several one-of-a-kind facilities and services. Celebrating its 50th anniversary this year, the 530-bed hospital is recognized as one of the "100 Most Wired" hospitals in America by Hospitals & Health Networks magazine. Memorial Health places emphasis on research, teaching and cutting-edge technology, making it a natural draw for many medical specialists to this area.

Candler Hospital, the oldest hospital in the state, joined with St. Joseph's Hospital, founded in 1875 by the Sisters of Mercy, to become a unified Health System in 1997, creating the largest healthcare provider in southeast Georgia and the South Carolina low country. While many services were consolidated, each facility has retained specialized components. The St. Joseph's campus is a 305-bed facility located on the south side of Savannah, which in addition to general services, offers treatment in a number of areas including cardiovascular, oncology, neurological and orthopedics services. The Candler campus is the second oldest continuously operating hospital in the United States. The 331-bed facility offers care in oncology, digestive diseases, pulmonology, outpatient surgery, and women's and children's services. The Children's Place is a comprehensive, acute-care pediatric unit.

St. Joseph's/Candler prides itself on being a faith-based hospital with special outreach programs such as The Screen Machine, a mobile cancer screening unit, that brings critical, affordable screenings to local residents, as well as support groups and health forums. The hospital is listed as one of the nation's top 100 Integrated Health Systems by Modern Health Care magazine.

In an ever-changing climate, both hospitals site financial performance as a critical issue for the area's medical caregivers, despite the combined budgets of Memorial Health and St. Joseph's/Candler's that top out at over $1 billion a year. Yet like all healthcare facilities, these two locally managed, not-for-profit hospitals face tremendous pressures like never before and are forced to come up with creative and effective means to create capital. As a result, the organizations' healthcare leaders, like many others across the nation, are putting their money into specialized care centers.

In the last four years, Memorial Health has built a 62,000-square-foot rehabilitation institute and a 27,500-square-foot cancer center, The Curtis and Elizabeth Anderson Cancer Institute, which is led by one of the most well-known gynecologic oncologists in the country, William J. Hoskins, M.D., formerly of Memorial Sloan-Kettering Cancer Center in New York. Additionally, there is a 13,750-square-foot internal medicine building, a child-care center and most recently, a $30 million, 189,000 square-foot facility, the Heart and Vascular Institute. The new center offers breakthrough technology that hosts some of the most comprehensive and technologically advanced cardiac and vascular services in the region. Those services include state-of-the-art surgical suites, catheterization labs, an electrophysiology lab, and angiography procedure rooms. The new Heart and Vascular Institute building will also be home to the region's first and only biplane angiography suite that will allow physicians to get a 3D image of the brain and actually see a stroke occurring.

Recruiting from among the nation's best, Memorial Health hires only board-certified physicians. Memorial Health University Physicians (MHUP) includes primary care physicians and more than 60 specialists who concentrate on everything from orthopedics to vascular surgery. Photos courtesy Memorial Health.

Savannah is renowned for its history, beauty, and hospitality. It is also becoming renowned as a center for exceptional healthcare. Memorial Health, headquartered on a 43-acre campus on Savannah's east side, serves a 35-county area in southeast Georgia and southern South Carolina. Memorial Health University Medical Center (MHUMC), a 530-bed teaching and research hospital, is the flagship of the organization, which is also home to the region's only children's hospital, Level 1 trauma center, and Level 3 neonatal intensive care nursery. Photos courtesy Memorial Health.

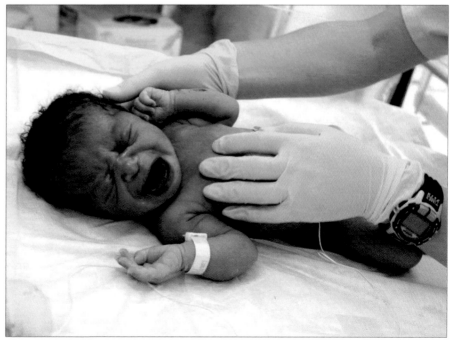

Likewise, St. Joseph's/Candler is home to the Heart Hospital, honing in on cardiovascular services that include full diagnostic and therapeutic treatment options such as medical cardiology, diagnostic and interventional cardiology, and cardiovascular and vascular surgery. In addition, the Heart Hospital offers comprehensive cardiovascular health primary and secondary preventive services, including cardiac disease screenings, risk reduction and wellness programs, and cardiac rehabilitation. The united Health System is also home to the areas only dedicated women's hospital - Mary Telfair Women's Hospital, which provides obstetrical, gynecological, education and outpatient services for women and also has specialized centers for digestive diseases and advanced bone and joint surgery. Most recently has been the construction of a $24 million, 56,000 square-foot free-standing facility, The Cancer Care & Research Pavilion. The center performs state-of-the-art medical procedures and precision-based technological advancements, focusing on clinical research, in conjunction with the NCI-designated H. Lee Moffitt Cancer Center and Research Institute, as well as prevention, treatment and follow-up care. Further plans include the "St. Joseph's/Candler Medical Office Park," an enclave of independent clinics that will act as informal partners to the hospital.

Wellness and prevention methods, like yoga, acupuncture, Reiki and aromatherapy, have become mainstay in Savannah's medical community as a way to enhance patients' overall well-being. With the intention to complement, not replace, traditional medicine, Memorial Health and St. Joseph's/Candler, along with numerous other holistic centers in Savannah are catering to the growing needs of individuals who are looking for alternative methods of care giving.

One example of that is The Chopra Center at Memorial Health, which was formed through a partnership with Deepak Chopra, M.D., a world-renowned figure on integrative medicine. The approach blends the best of medical science with mind-body techniques to help people reduce stress and take charge of their overall health. St. Joseph's/Candler's Cancer Care and Research Pavilion provides similar treatments to soothe the mind, body and spirit. Cancer patients can make use of a boutique that offers wigs, turbans and prostheses, to help with the physical and emotional changes that occur. The boutique is staffed by cancer survivors who offer advice and inspiration through their own stories. The Pavilion also offers music therapy and pet therapy.

A competitive local hospital market is ultimately what drives the area's hospitals to be considered some of the best in the country today. But Savannah's pioneering efforts date back to the city's founder, British General James Oglethorpe and a hand-picked group of scholars and doctors who arrived with him in Savannah in 1733.

One of the first noted references to medical care in Savannah is that of Elizabeth Warren, who lived on the northeast corner of Whitaker and Bryan Streets and set up an infirmary in her home in 1734. By March of 1737, however, one of Georgia's trustees, Viscount Percival, addressed the need for medical attention for orphans and the sick and, taking heed, George Whitfield, a minister, established Bethesda Orphanage in 1740. The institution housed a hospital and free clinic.

The end of the Colonial Period brought a new kind of hospital, the lazaretto, or better known as a quarantine station. The Act of 1749, which permitted the importation of slaves, called for the creation of a lazaretto on Tybee Island. Quarantine regulations stated that all of those arriving ill were to remain on-board and treated there and the dead were buried in unmarked graves. Such practices continued through The War Between the States, until condemnation shortly thereafter and a new station was established elsewhere.

Most of Savannah's economy was based largely on plantation crops and foreign trade, making this area one of great wealth. Therefore, Georgia State Legislature passed an act of trade in 1789 with a tax provision of three pence per ton on all shipping that entered Savannah's port. This fund was set aside for a hospital for sick and disabled seamen, both black and white. A Board of Commissioners was appointed by the Georgia Legislature to oversee the hospital in Savannah.

Further, the Savannah business elite began making progressive measures in the city's expansion and made it their mission to lure well educated physicians to settle in Georgia. The citizens of Savannah were also very interested in improving the existing standard of medicine and in 1774 approached the Legislature about forming a lottery that would fund a poor house and hospital.

An initial $10,000 was raised by private citizens and the City Council allotted space for a new building to be raised at East Broad and Broughton Streets. However, the building was never erected and it took more than 20 years to see the true fruits of their labor.

In 1808 a brick building in Yamacraw, formerly the Federal jail, was purchased, with $3,000 in aid from City Council. The Savannah Poor House and Hospital was officially chartered, yet funds were still needed. It would be seven more years before a building would be designed for the hospital, following two more lotteries and other private monies. The Savannah Poor House and Hospital later opened its new building in 1820, but between a fire that burned 163 homes and the Yellow Fever epidemic, Savannah's population declined from 6,000 to 1,494 in rapid succession, and the hospital, along with the city, suffered greatly. Then in 1835, the hospital was privatized and chartered under the State of Georgia and funded by private contributions, interest on assets owned and yearly state auction taxes.

Coinciding with the new hospital in 1808 was the formation of the Georgia Medical Society, which today is the oldest County Medical Society in existence in the United States. Savannah's citizenry was resplendent with highly educated doctors, who saw Savannah as a beautiful, yet potentially hazardous city, due to the climate and exposure of diseases. This group of doctors took it upon themselves to approach the Legislature of the State of Georgia to charter the Georgia Medical Society in Savannah for the purpose of "lessening the fatality induced by the climate and incidental causes, and improving the science of medicine."

The Georgia Medical Society became an integral component of the newly founded Savannah Poor House and Hospital, assisting in the hiring of staff and lobbying efforts on behalf of physicians. As the society has evolved over the years, it has always offered educational programs for the community. There are roughly 500 members today who practice in Chatham, Effingham, Bryan, McIntosh and Long counties.

In the years following the establishment of the hospital and the medical society, the Georgia Infirmary was chartered on December 24, 1832, by Thomas Francis Williams, a minister and landowner. The first medical facility of its kind in the country, it was founded "for the relief and protection of afflicted and aged Africans," after an incident in January, 1816, that left the Reverend Williams outraged and condemned from his church.

One of the men in his congregation at the First Baptist Church, located at Montgomery and Bryan Streets, severely beat two of his slaves, one of whom died. At that time the vestrymen of the church were charged with trying anyone who had broken the law. A known advocate of justice, Reverend Williams saw to it that the slaves were allowed to testify in the case, an unusual privilege for slaves.

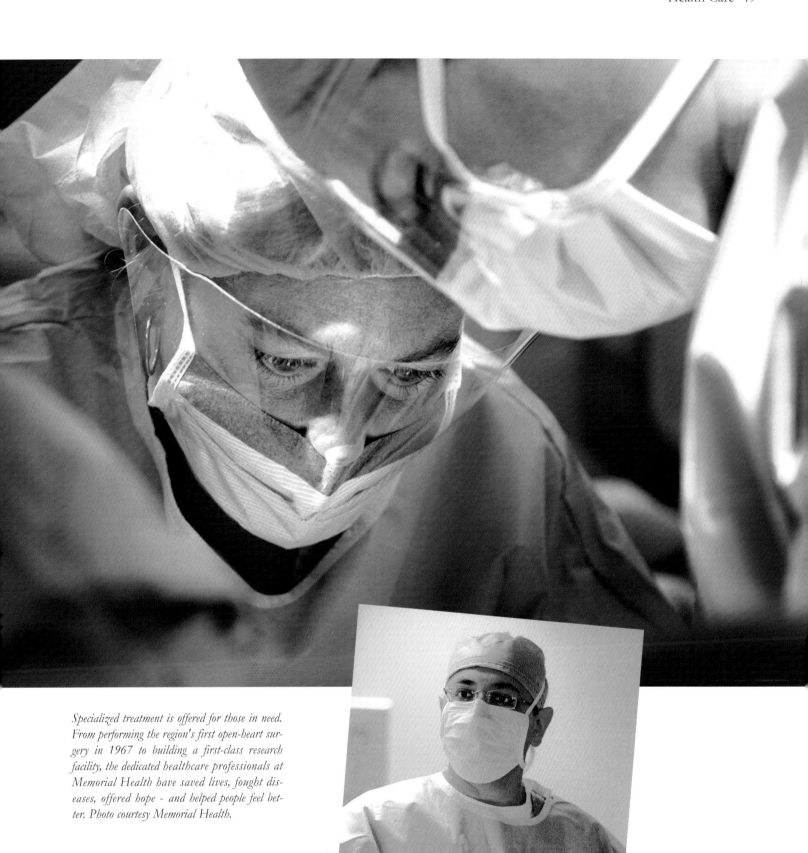

Specialized treatment is offered for those in need. From performing the region's first open-heart surgery in 1967 to building a first-class research facility, the dedicated healthcare professionals at Memorial Health have saved lives, fought diseases, offered hope - and helped people feel better. Photo courtesy Memorial Health.

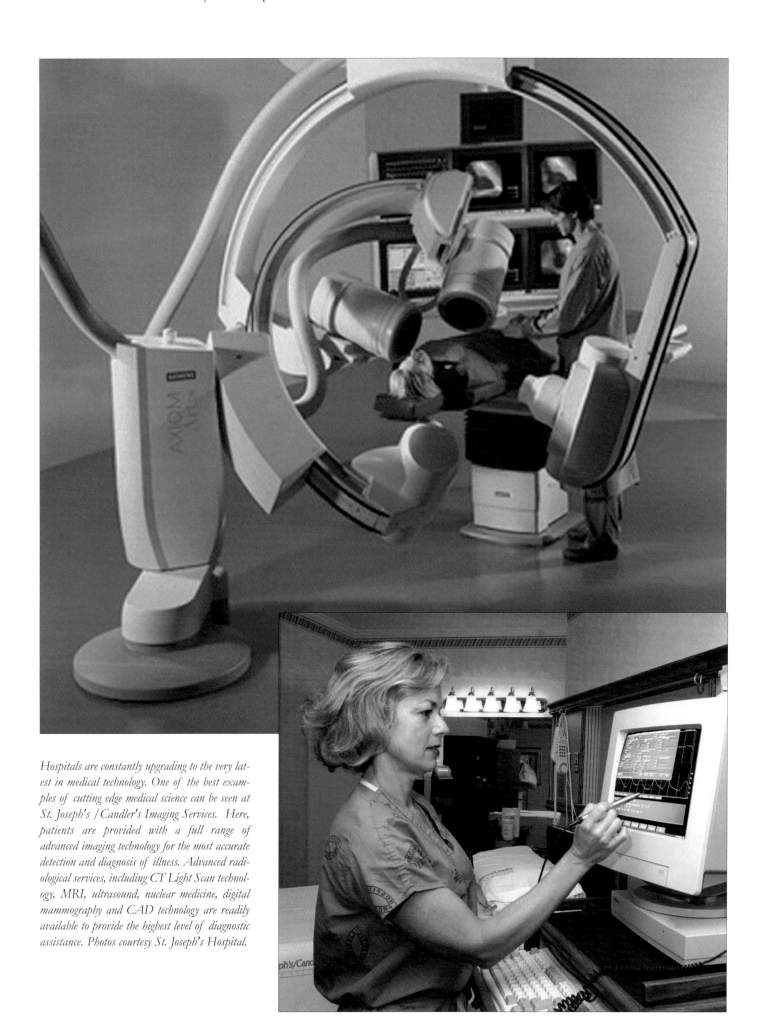

Hospitals are constantly upgrading to the very latest in medical technology. One of the best examples of cutting edge medical science can be seen at St. Joseph's /Candler's Imaging Services. Here, patients are provided with a full range of advanced imaging technology for the most accurate detection and diagnosis of illness. Advanced radiological services, including CT Light Scan technology, MRI, ultrasound, nuclear medicine, digital mammography and CAD technology are readily available to provide the highest level of diagnostic assistance. Photos courtesy St. Joseph's Hospital.

The slave owner was found innocent and the minister, horrified by what had happened, refused to return to his congregation. He was ex-communicated and died a month later, leaving his money to establish the Georgia Infirmary. However, it wasn't until 1832 that his brother, Richard F. Williams, actually opened its doors on a tract of land next to Bethesda. In later years it was moved into the city, on 14 acres bound by what are today Bull, 37th, 35th and Lincoln streets. Slave owners who sent patients made small contributions to help fund the infirmary, which remained open through the end of the Civil War.

However, by 1865, the assets of the infirmary were seized, except for the land, which stayed under the control of the Trustees. In 1871, a local merchant made a donation of $10,000 to re-open the institution's doors, which provided the only source of medical attention for African-Americans in the area. In 1904 a training school for "colored" nurses opened and the first class graduated in 1906. In a monumental move, the infirmary opened to all individuals in 1964, but ultimately encountered its demise after the introduction of desegregation and Medicare, which allowed patients to seek healthcare elsewhere. The public began entering other hospitals like Candler General (now St. Joseph's/Candler) and Memorial Medical Center (now Memorial Health University Medical Center) and the Infirmary, which was self-supporting, could not compete. The infirmary did later re-open as Georgia's first day center for stroke rehabilitation in 1975, with grants from Candler Hospital and the Community Cardiovascular Council Inc. and in 2004 celebrated a $3.2 million dollar renovation, funded by St. Joseph's/Candler, Georgia Infirmary Trustees and individual donations. The non-profit organization today cares for elderly and physically disabled patients.

From War and Devastation to Prosperous Modern Times Savannah on the whole was a city pinched by wars, which in turn, made heavy use of the existing services for soldiers.

In 1863, the hospital was used as a Confederate Hospital until Sherman's siege. After the Union army left, the hospital was left with nothing and the building was used by African-American refugees until 1866. Whereupon, at that time, Dr. William Duncan, the president of the hospital, received a grant of $4,000 to re-open the center. In 1872, the facility was renamed Savannah Hospital with care limited to the sick and in 1876 the yellow fever epidemic hit, devastating the city. The story goes that a tunnel was built under the parking lot adjacent to the hospital, reportedly so that victims could be removed from the hospital by the underground passage and placed in the woods of Forsyth Park. Officials were trying to prevent mass hysteria amongst the locals, who would have likely panicked at the sight of the seriousness of the disease.

Just one year prior to the yellow fever outbreak, in 1875, St. Joseph's Infirmary was founded by His Excellency Bishop William H. Gross of Savannah. At Gross' request, Sister Mary Cecilia Carroll from the Savannah Institute of the Sisters of Mercy was officiated as the superintendent of this new hospital. She, along with four other Sisters, began in a twelve-room, wooden home on East Broad and Gordon Streets where they had to reach the second floor, laden with medicines, soaps, towels and water basins, by climbing a rope ladder, to care for the 'colored' patients who were housed in the attic. Without modern day conveniences, the Sisters were forced to draw water from an outdoor pump and heat it on a wood stove before taking it to patients. Eight months later the infirmary moved to the corner of Habersham and Taylor streets and in 1901 the first addition was made to the hospital and the name was officially changed to St. Joseph's Hospital.

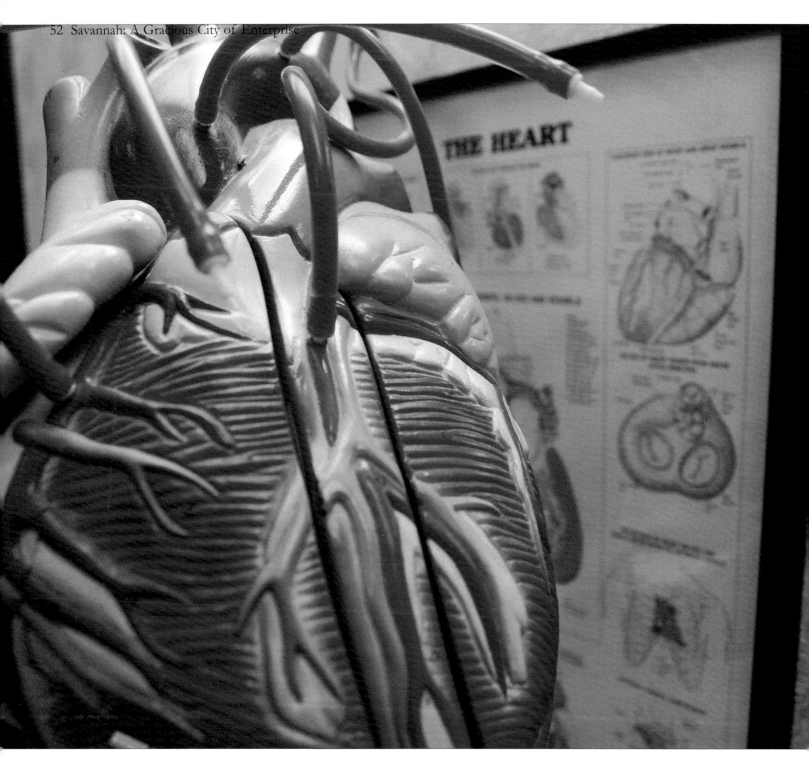

St. Joseph's is home to The Heart Hospital, The Institute for Advanced Bone and Joint Surgery and the Institute of Neurosciences, each offering unsurpassed space-age technology and expert clinical care. St. Joseph's/Candler is involved in multiple clinical research studies in the areas of pulmonary, endocrinology, cardiology, pediatrics, rheumatology, oncology, surgery, ENT and orthopedics. St. Joseph's/Candler's modern, futuristic approach to technology, assists physicians, surgeons and clinical staff in providing the patient with only the highest quality of care. Photos courtesy St. Joseph's.

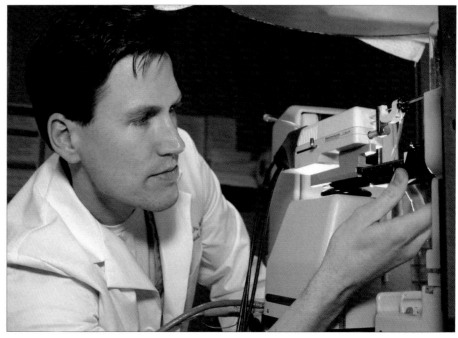

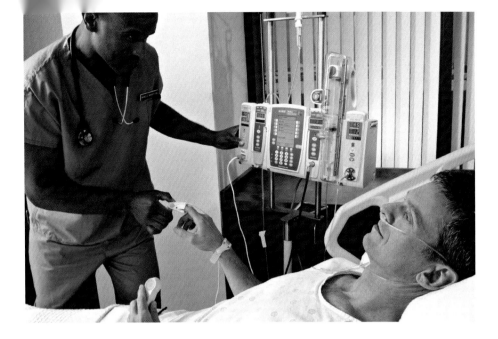

Other healthcare facilities were erected. The Telfair Hospital, willed into existence by philanthropist Mary Telfair, daughter of a wealthy merchant-planter and governor of Georgia, cared specifically for sick, indigent women and children. The Charity Hospital began in 1893 in the private home of Drs. Cornelius and Woodby McKane, an African-American husband-and-wife team. They also went on to create a nursing school for black nurses, re-chartering and changing the hospital's name to the Charity Hospital and Training School for Nurses.

Within the first half of the twentieth century three more hospitals emerged in Savannah, one of which was the U.S. Marine Hospital, set up in 1906 by the U.S. Public Health Service. Another was the Oglethorpe Sanitarium, which opened in 1908 as a private hospital owned by Dr. John Daniel, who addressed the needs of rest-cure patients, an antiquated term for what would now be referred to as exhaustion, depression or perhaps plain boredom. Several years later, in1927, the Central of Georgia Railway also opened a hospital for its employees.

The Depression left public support of Savannah Hospital to a minimum and a committee formed to recommend that the city should sell its interest in the hospital to the Methodists, who had already shown great interest in the local healthcare system. Under the leadership of Bishop Warren A. Candler, the Methodist Church acquired the hospital for $1,000 on December 20, 1930, and changed the institution's name again, this time to Warren A. Candler Hospital. In 1965 the name would change once more to Candler General Hospital, Inc. after absorbing The Mary Telfair and the Central of Georgia Railway Hospitals.

In 1946, Congress had passed the Hospital Survey and Construction Act, sponsored by Senators Lister Hill and Harold Burton, widely known as the Hill-Burton Act. It was the nation's major health facility construction program that was originally designed to provide federal grants to modernize hospitals which had become obsolete due to lack of capital investment throughout the period of the Great Depression and World War II (1929 to 1945).

Under this act, funds were provided to the Telfair, St. Joseph's and the Warren Candler Hospitals, but there were still many locals who could foresee a problem if the medical facilities did not unite. There were concerns that the string of individual hospitals was not adequate for their growing community. Many concluded that what Savannah needed was one large, central institution that would accommodate all of the medical divisions.

Therefore, in 1946, a hospital committee from the Georgia Medical Society was created to act in the best interests of all medical groups, with the ultimate goal of finding the most appropriate hospitalization system for the city.

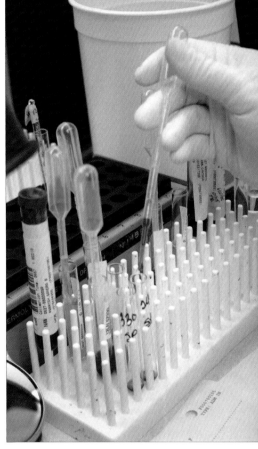

An underlying philosophy at St. Joseph's/Candler is to remain ahead of the technology curve. Access to the latest advancements in research, treatment and technology are paramount ingredients to successful patient outcomes and the overall patient experience. Photo courtesy St. Joseph's.

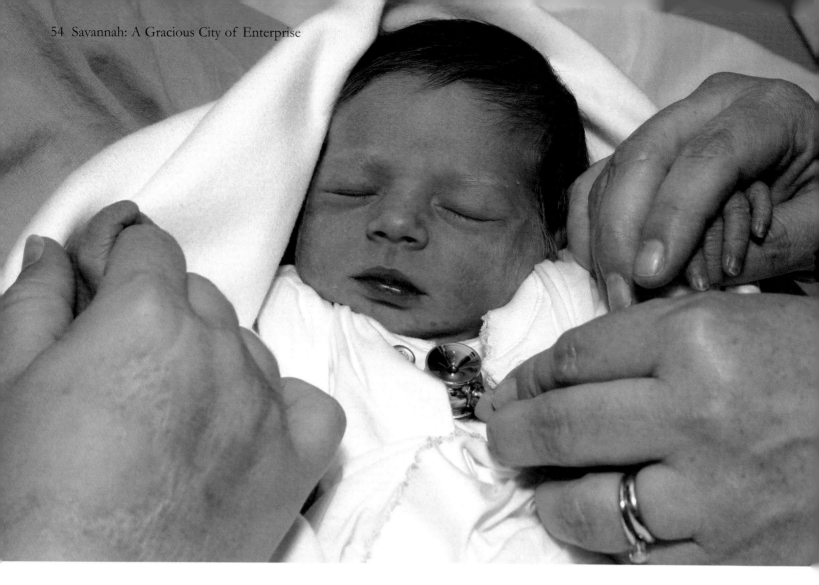

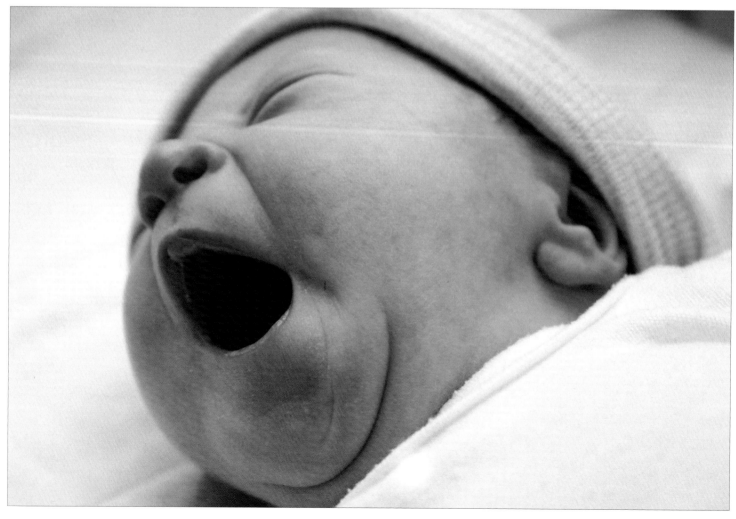

At the same time, several veterans' associations also decided to create a living memorial in honor of those who had died in battle. They appointed a Memorial Committee that joined forces with the Medical Society's hospital committee, adding a powerful punch to the plea for a general hospital. Savannah's citizens on the whole were ecstatic at the prospect, as were the city's mayor and other local government officials.

Savannah wasn't eligible for Hill-Burton funds until 1952-53, but strident research efforts were made until those would be available. Once the city was able to collect the federal monies, the county took responsibility for the operation of the hospital and elected a board of directors.

Land was purchased in 1953 and the hospital was officially opened and dedicated in1955. The new Memorial Hospital opened as a 300-bed general hospital dedicated as a living memorial to the nation's war dead. Revenues were funded by several sources including the Hill-Burton Act, a grant from the state of Georgia and a $100,000 gift from Union Bag and Paper Corporation in Savannah.

Memorial Hospital went on to sign an agreement with the Medical College of Georgia, establishing Memorial as a teaching hospital and in 1985 the hospital formed its own governing body and became Memorial Medical Center (MMC). That same year the hospital joined with Savannah McDonald's restaurant co-op to form a non-profit organization to establish and operate a Ronald McDonald House, an outfit that serves families of pediatric patients from southeastern Georgia and southern South Carolina.

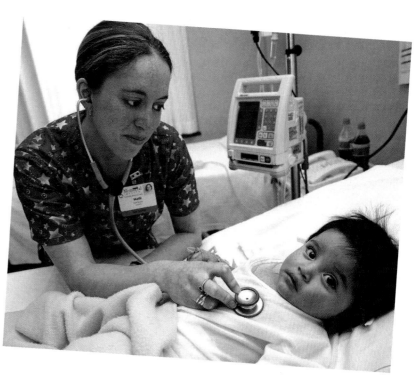

In 1999 the hospital changed its name for the last time to Memorial Health University Medical Center. As southeast Georgia's only teaching and research hospital, the Medical Center is now also affiliated with the Mercer University School of Medicine and in 2000 the George and Marie Backus Children's Hospital at Memorial Health was approved as a primary research site for the Children's Cancer Group, the nation's largest children's cancer study organization. That same year, Memorial Health sponsored and provided sports medicine coverage for the USA weightlifting team in the 2000 Summer Olympics in Sydney, Australia. Most recently, the hospital was named as one of the "50 Exceptional U.S. Hospitals" for Patient Safety, in a report published in the April 2005 issue of Consumers Digest magazine.

Savannah's medical community is booming like never before. Today there are more than 1,300 hospital beds, nearly 650 physicians and surgeons, 1,600 plus registered nurses, almost 200 dentists and numerous alternative medical facilities to serve the Savannah metro area and beyond. The combination of new technology, a competitive hospital environment and an aging population have jointly fueled excellent patient care for the 35-county region, spanning 3,200 miles. With access to comprehensive and specialized services, Savannah's residents are privy to essential and urgent care without ever having to leave the city.

In 1985 Memorial Health hospital joined with Savannah McDonald's restaurant co-op to form a non-profit organization to establish and operate a Ronald McDonald House, an outfit that serves families of pediatric patients from southeastern Georgia and southern South Carolina. Top photo courtesy Memorial Health.

Candler Hospital is home to the Mary Telfair Women's Hospital, the region's undisputed leader in advanced obstetrical, gynecological, education and outpatient services for women. Opposite page photos courtesy St Joseph's.

CHAPTER FOUR

Education Bright Minds

By Melanie Simón

Savannah has always been a pioneer in education. Today, the coastal city is aggressively rebuilding and improving its public school system and offers some of the finest private schools in the state, as well as nationally recognized higher education institutions. Savannah is home to two colleges that are part of the state's University System and one private college, The Savannah College of Art and Design, that is the largest art school in the nation. The world-class Georgia Institute of Technology, known here as Georgia Tech Savannah, is expanding its engineering education opportunities locally, making this region highly desirable for knowledge-based industries looking to recruit graduates.

Savannah offers some of the finest private schools in the state. St. Andrew's School, is located

on Wilmington Island, and prides itself on individual attention. In the public school system there are 29

quality pre-kindergarten programs offered for eligible 4-year-old children.

Photo courtesy St Andrew's School.

With an enrollment of more than 36,000 students in 48 facilities, The Savannah-Chatham County Public Schools system is by far the largest stakeholder on the local education scene. No other school district in Georgia has made stronger gains in overall academic performance over the last three years than the public school system. Through the promotion of innovation, creativity and exploration into excelled academics, the arts, technology, engineering, math, foreign language and marine science, the Savannah-Chatham County Public Academy/Magnet Schools system has become a draw for students and parents across the county. The most recent addition has been an Engineering Academy, the first of its kind in the state of Georgia, for elementary school students. Area business leaders, like Gulfstream Aerospace and Great Dane are taking an active role in the curriculum development for the school.

The 21st century brings about education opportunities that benefit both parent and child. There are currently many schools that allow parents to monitor their children's academic careers online. Facilitating easy communication with teachers via e-mail, parents can check homework assignments, see attendance records, view grades and school announcements. One can also receive automatic e-mail notification of tardy or unexcused absences, missing assignments, failing grades or discipline incidents.

In the public school system there are 29 quality pre-kindergarten programs offered for eligible 4-year-old children, five full days per week, for 36 weeks per year. Kindergarten programs are available at 31 elementary schools, with a full curriculum that is designed to build a solid foundation in all subjects.

The founders of the Savannah College of Art and Design had vision, and some say a lot of chutzpah, but they never imagined that in just 26 years their idea would flourish to encompass 7,500 students, 10,000 alumni, three campuses and virtual classrooms via the Internet. They just wanted to make a difference in the lives of aspiring artists. SCAD is the largest art school in the nation. Photo courtesy SCVB.

The Skidaway Institute of Oceanography (SkIO) is an autonomous research unit of the University System of Georgia. Their mission being to provide access to marine research facilities in a nationally and internationally recognized center of excellence in marine science. Photo courtesy Skidaway Institute of Oceanography.

Eleven middle schools, including Georgia's first charter school, nine high schools and nine educational centers are located in the public school district.

Recent advances, like a $221 million building program that funded 13 new schools, opened between the summer of 1996 and 2003, have been instrumental in higher academic testing scores and attracting highly qualified instructors, as the Savannah-Chatham County Public Schools system leads the state in the number of teachers with National Board Certification.

Each elementary, middle, and high school in the Savannah-Chatham County Public School system offers instructional services through SEARCH, Students Exploring And Reasoning for Creative Horizons, as part of the gifted program for the school district. SEARCH students in kindergarten through eighth grade earn an appropriate grade on a nine-week report card. Secondary students receive grades in advanced level classes, Advanced Placement classes, and a variety of elective credit options.

Students in the public school system also have the ability to learn modern and classical languages, such as Latin, Spanish, French, and German. Instructors are all state certified and students can participate in language competitions, bilingual plays, and dance and musical performances.

Some high schools offer the International Baccalaureate (IB) Program, a rigorous academic curriculum for eleventh and twelfth grade students, recognized for college credit by higher education institutions in the United States. High school students may also participate in Advanced Placement (AP) language programs. They may receive college credit if their AP standardized test scores meet the criteria set by their selected colleges.

Arts education plays an important part of the curriculum of the schools. All of the elementary schools offer general music classes and visual art classes for the students, and band classes for fifth graders. Yamaha MIE Piano Keyboard Labs are available in most of the elementary schools for state-of-the-art computerized music technology. String instruments, dance and theater are also offered at the Bloomingdale and Gadsden Academy programs.

Middle school and high school students have the option of continuing their studies in the visual and performing arts through band, chorus, and visual art classes. Drama instruction is available at several middle schools and high schools, and students may elect to audition for the Academy at Shuman Middle School for instruction in art, music, dance and theater. Any student who has a serious interest in the arts can audition for the Savannah Arts Academy, a dedicated arts high school where all students select a major in one or more arts disciplines.

Through many changes over a 75 year period, Armstrong Atlantic has stayed true to its rich tradition, focusing on a firm commitment to the ideals of a liberal education. As a result, the university has graduated many who are now the region's leading attorneys, businessmen, physicians, scientists, healthcare professionals, a mayor, eighty percent of local nurses and non-physician medical staff, and over half of the area's Teachers of the Year. Photos courtesy Armstrong Atlantic.

Business and technology are also heavily emphasized with those as young as sixth grade so that students will be well-versed in advancing technology, marketing and entrepreneurship from a young age.

Those efforts are exemplified through the Youth Apprenticeship Program (YAP), a school and work-based learning program for high school juniors and seniors who wish to work with local business leaders and gain experience in the real workforce.

The school system also aggressively pursues business partnerships throughout Savannah, as a way to help strengthen the community, with the notion that today's students are tomorrow's leaders.

Recently, the public school system partnered with YMCA of Coastal Georgia and the Savannah Chatham Youth Futures Authority to petition the State Board of Education for a 21st Century Community Learning Centers grant for the 2004-2005 school year. The grant was awarded for almost $1.4 million. The three year total will amount to more than $4 million and will be eligible to apply for grant continuation awards for two more years. The grant establishes eight 21st Century Community Learning Center sites, which will serve high-poverty students who are enrolled at low-performing schools. Students who have not met reading and math standards in the most recent testing will be targeted for participation in the program, with tutorials and other academic enrichment activities to be provided for those students.

As for private schools, there has been a surge in the local private school sector, especially Catholic schools, in line with an influx of new fundamentalist Christian schools across the U.S. in recent years. Academies like Savannah Country Day School, which is one of the oldest private schools in continuous operation in Savannah, are also quite popular.

There are 24 private schools serving the area with programs that offer a variety of learning opportunities. The facilities promote classes in pre-kindergarten through the twelfth grade and range in size from 250 students to almost 1,500. Annual tuition costs are as low as $1,800 and as high as $12,500. Many of the schools are Christian in nature, but others take a purely secular approach. In general, the institutions that have high school programs focus more on the students' preparation for college.

Savannah Country Day School offers honors curriculum, Advance Placement, foreign language instruction beginning in the third grade and its students are consistently recognized by The National Merit Scholarship Corporation. The average SAT scores for the last three graduating classes is 1283 and travel to Spain, Costa Rica, Quebec and France is scheduled for reinforcement and cultural awareness.

St. Vincent's Academy is another landmark educational institution in Savannah, having opened its doors in 1845. Founded by the Sisters of Mercy, it is one of the oldest private schools in the state. As a Catholic school for girls, the facility educates nearly 400 students of all religious faiths on the downtown campus. With comprehensive courses in the arts, sciences and humanities and an extensive athletic program, St. Vincent's prepares girls for college preparatory curriculum.

The world-class Georgia Institute of Technology, known here as Georgia Tech Savannah, is expanding its engineering education opportunities locally, making this region highly desirable for knowledge-based industries looking to recruit graduates. Photo courtesy SEDA.

Opposite page: Savannah Technical College has been meeting the needs of its community for 75 years, as the area's leading provider of high-quality, industry-driven technical education. After five years of explosive growth in enrollment, the College now serves 4,000 students each quarter in Bryan, Chatham, Effingham and Liberty Counties, offering more than 50 certificate, diploma and associate degree programs in allied health, business and applied manufacturing. Photo courtesy Savannah Technical College.

Savannah Christian Preparatory School (SCPS) is an independent, non-denominational, college prep Christian school that seeks partnerships with families, churches and the local community to educate through Christ-centered training, application and example. The school presently maintains two campuses. The 254-acre Chatham Parkway campus hosts nearly 1,000 Lower and Upper School students and 160 Daycare/Pre-school students. Facilities include thirteen buildings with classrooms, labs, media centers, a gym, and a cafeteria, an outdoor pool, a track, five athletic fields, three playgrounds, and the Ecological Diversity for Educational Networking (E.D.E.N.) outdoor education center.

Another 14-acre campus is home to over 500 Lower and Middle School students. Facilities include four buildings with classrooms, labs, media centers, a cafeteria, and two gyms, as well as two athletic fields.

The island communities are represented by such schools as St. Andrew's School, located on Wilmington Island, which emphasizes a curriculum designed to help students reach their full potential as scholars, athletes, artists, and leaders. The school prides itself on individual attention and finding students hidden talents.

As well, St. Michael's School, which serves grades kindergarten through eight, is the only school on Tybee Island and has been meeting the needs of island children since 1948. It is a Catholic school, offering high academic achievement, a full sports program, planned social events and a modest tuition.

With a full range of opportunities and choices, Savannah's private and public schools need not but look to the city's founding fathers, who planted the city's roots with a strong foundation bordered around the importance of education.

The island communities are represented by such schools as St. Andrew's School, located on Wilmington Island, which emphasizes a curriculum designed to help students reach their full potential as scholars, athletes, artists, and leaders. Photos courtesy St Andrew's School.

Moving Forward

Today, the Board of Public Education takes enormous strides to see that all students are treated equally and fairly and excel in reading, language arts, mathematics, sciences and technology. With the help of the magnet program, students are reaching new heights, like never before.

Middle and high school principals are also now working together very closely, to ensure consistency patterns for both children and parents, as they make the move to from middle to high school. There are many efforts being made for redistricting lines that would ensure that students would move from elementary to middle to high school together, with a goal of creating a networking and bonding system for students and parents alike.

The higher education system in Savannah boasts exemplary facilities and technology to keep with a city that is growing on a rapid basis. Nationally recognized institutions like Georgia Tech and The Savannah College of Art and Design have put Savannah on the educational map with their world-renowned programs in engineering and art, respectively.

There are also a plethora of state and independent learning institutions that educate in all areas. Armstrong Atlantic State University, which is acclaimed for academic excellence since its founding in 1935, is affiliated with the University System of Georgia. The university offers undergraduate and graduate degrees in more than 75 programs through the colleges of Arts and Sciences, Education and Health Professions, the School of Computing, and the School of Graduate Studies.

Benedictine Military School is a private, military, all male high school, in Savannah, Georgia. Founded in 1902 by Benedictine monks and has a rich tradition rooted in what is quintisential Savannah. Photos courtesy Benedictine Military School.

Savannah State University offers 22 undergraduate degree programs through the colleges of Science and Technology, Business Administration, and Arts and Sciences. Masters degrees in public administration, social work, urban studies, and marine science are also available.

The Savannah Technical College, which has been in existence for nearly 75 years, offers more than 50 professional diploma and associate degree programs in fields ranging from automotive technology to surgical technology and from marketing to computer information systems and allied health programs.

South University was created in 1899 in Savannah as a business college, and became a four-year institution in 1996, when the Bachelor of Business Administration degree program was added to the curricula. Bachelors degrees in information technology and legal studies are offered, as is a masters degree in physician assistant studies.

All in all, Savannah's educational system facilitates excellence from a child's beginning years to an adult's continuing education and makes every effort that today's students will be able to meet the changing needs of our regional and national economy.

Savannah Technical College, through its commitment to quality, service and responsiveness to its community, remains an integral force in the growth and development of southeast Georgia. Savannah Technical College is accredited by the Southern Association of Colleges and Schools to award the associate degree. Photo courtesy Savannah Technical College.

CHAPTER   FIVE

The
Good Life

By   Allison Hersch

Savannah's beauty crowns the Georgia coast. From a vantage point atop a bluff, she gracefully presides over the silver waters of the Savannah River as it flows calmly toward its fate. Amid the natural bounty of the Lowcountry, she has provided a handsome home to generations and a gracious welcome to the countless visitors who seek her out.

Appropriately dubbed the "Belle of Georgia," Savannah is a city of many moods. She is indisputably charming and hospitable, but those who know her intimately can tell you that she is also downright provocative on occasion. Savannah is elegant, patient and, sometimes, just a little bit naughty. Everything about her, especially her strength, is refined. Savannah can be sultry at times. She has been known to inspire great passion. She thrives on admiration and secretly cherishes eccentricity. Wearing her distinctive architecture, genteel streets and picturesque gardens like a string of pearls, she continues to captivate in beautiful style.

Families, college students and retiree's are among those who are proud to call the downtown area home.

In the morning, they may walk their dogs in the city's squares or greet their neighbors from the shade of a

magnolia tree, but several times a year they come together in the continuing effort to preserve the quality

of life in Savannah's National Landmark Historic District. Photo courtesy SCVB.

Each December, the Downtown Neighborhood Association hosts a popular Holiday Home Tour. Savannah's citizen's decorate with red ribbons, greenery & glitter.

Savannah is known for its unique Dolphin down spouts.

In fact, Savannah is remarkably well-preserved for her age. Unlike so many of her southern sisters, she was famously spared the harsh treatment meted out by General William Tecumseh Sherman. Age finally began to take its toll, however. The city and its people suffered from the collapse of the cotton industry in the 1920s and the subsequent strain of the Great Depression. Following World War II, Savannah flirted with development in an attempt to revive her faded glory. Fortunately, she had friends she could count on.

Flying firmly in the face of the urban renewal movement that was sweeping the country in the 1950s, a group of determined women established the Historic Savannah Foundation. Since its inception, the Foundation has not only preserved much of Savannah's historic architecture but has gone a long way in preserving its timeless charm as well. In 1966, Savannah's Historic District was designated a National Historic Landmark. Today, it remains one of the largest historic landmarks in the country.

From the stately grandeur of its cobblestone streets to the urban elegance of the antique shops on Bull Street, the National Landmark Historic District attracts millions of tourists every year. It has also attracted the attention of the editors of Robb Report magazine, who named Savannah the American city with the most exceptional architecture in the 2005 edition of its annual "Best Places to Live" feature. The advantages of living in Savannah, however, are old news to residents who have enjoyed walking to City Market, River Street and Forsyth Park for years.

Forsyth Park, with its 20 plus acres, is the largest park in Savannah. It is graced with an exquisite, landmark, cast-iron white fountain styled in 1858 after one that embodies the Place de la Concorde in Paris. Forsyth Park has often been the scene for Civil War re-enactments and is a popular location for the shooting of such films as Forest Gump and Midnight in the Garden of Good and Evil. The park is frequently crowded with active students with their pets and Frisbees, along with sports enthusiasts brushing up on their touch football, basketball, tennis and softball, alongside families enjoying picnics and weddings.

A plentiful mix of antique shops, and secret gardens add charm to the historic district. Photos courtesy SCVB.

Forsyth Park was laid out by the city in 1851, and is named for Georgia Governor, John Forsyth. The 20 acre park is especially beautiful in the spring when the azaleas are bursting with colorful blossoms. Photos courtesy SCVB.

Savannah's National Landmark Historic District encompasses hip urban lofts on Broughton Street as well as elegant antebellum mansions on Gaston Street. Waterfront penthouses on River Street offer a prime view of the ships that glide down the Savannah River while historic town homes on Jones Street nestle beneath the shade of live oak trees. A plentiful mix of restaurants, boutiques, historic inns and antique shops add sparkle, charm and variety to the life of the district.

Families, college students and retiree's are among those who are proud to call the downtown area home. In the morning, they may walk their dogs in the city's squares or greet their neighbors from the shade of a magnolia tree, but several times a year they come together in the continuing effort to preserve the quality of life in Savannah's National Landmark Historic District. Each December, the Downtown Neighborhood Association hosts a popular Holiday Home Tour, which raises money for historic preservation. The annual Home and Garden Tour offers a similar opportunity to see some of the city's finest homes each spring.

Chippewa
Square

Savannah's diverse and spectacular beauty charm photographers and couples alike with endless possibilities.

Famous for the James Oglethorpe monument Chippewa Square is located in Savannah's historic district. The trees are draped with Spanish moss and offer shade on a warm afternoon. Photo courtesy SCVB.

Picturesque Madison Square with flowering blue pansy's. Designed in 1837 and named for James Madison. The square is home to a monument in honor of Sgt. William Jasper, hero of the siege of Savannah in 1779.

The Olde Pink House, built on a land grant from the British Crown was once a branch of the Bank of the United States. Today it is a popular restaurant noted by locals for its fine dining and romantic atmosphere. Magnificent architecture, historic inns and a variety of restaurants, boutiques and flowers are part of Savannah's charm.

The National Landmark Historic District may be the jewel in Savannah's crown, but the city is comprised of an intricate patchwork quilt of neighborhoods, each with its own distinctive history and character. Some areas have ties to the ocean, while others trace their roots back to Savannah's earliest days.

Often referred to as "Savannah's first suburb," the Victorian District originally developed as an extension of the Landmark Historic District. It has enjoyed a renaissance in the past decade as many of the large frame homes erected around the turn of the previous century on Waldburg Street, Park Avenue, Henry Street and Anderson Street have been given a new lease on life. Orderly tree-lined streets, a convenient midtown location and a line-up of well-respected public schools have made Ardsley Park popular with families. At its heart, Hull Park serves as a popular gathering place for children's birthday parties, play dates and picnics. Ardsley Park, with its grid of landscaped squares, was originally planned in 1910 as a twentieth-century extension of and variation on Oglethorpe's original city plan. Chatham Crescent, on the other hand, serves as a rare example of Southern Beaux Arts design with its crescent-shaped avenues and small circular parks.

Isle of Hope is another family-friendly neighborhood. Narrow, oak-lined streets hint at the community's roots, which date back to 1736. Located approximately 15 miles south of downtown Savannah, the Isle of Hope National Historic District includes the river view homes of some of Georgia's earliest colonists as well as the residences built along scenic Bluff Drive in the nineteenth century by Savannah's elite in an attempt to escape from the trials of summer heat and malaria.

Skidaway Island has long been known for its remarkable natural beauty and exclusive gated communities. Increasingly, newer gated communities, such as The Landings and Southbridge, as well as suburban Southside neighborhoods like Georgetown and Windsor Forest are providing comfortable new options for Savannah residents. In addition to historic charm, homeowners can now take advantage of easy access to shopping and transportation, enhanced privacy, award-winning golf courses and a country club lifestyle.

No matter what part of the city you call your own, you're in a perfect position to enjoy the good life in Savannah. From graceful Regency town homes with a view of history to villas that overlook peaceful fairways, Savannah is undeniably gracious at home. When it's time to play, however, this Southern Belle is always ready to put her best foot forward.

Beneath the city's live oak canopy, a diverse cultural scene is flourishing. Under the stars, the hottest restaurants, bistros and night spots tempt visitors and residents alike to sample the city's distinctive flavor. Charming shops, scattered like pearls along the city's streets, have been touted in the pages of Vogue. Music fills the air, festivals fill the calendar and the stage is always set for entertainment.

Savannah celebrates music, art, culture and food with more than 150 festivals every year. From the annual Martin Luther King, Jr. Parade in January to the Festival of Trees and Lights in December, special events, fairs and fetes fuel the good life all year long. In March, half a million revelers don green and take to the streets for the city's annual St. Patrick's Day celebration, one of the largest in the country. In June, the Blessing of the Fleet and Seafood Harvest Festival is held. The Tybee Kite Festival lifts the city's spirits in November.

In March, half a million revelers don green and take to the streets for the city's annual St. Patrick's Day celebration, one of the largest in the country. In June, the Blessing of the Fleet and Seafood Harvest Festival is held. Photos SCVB.

Music fills the air, festivals fill the calendar and the stage is always set for entertainment. The Savannah Music Festival tops the agenda for 17 days every March. Photo courtesy SCVB.

The Savannah Music Festival tops the agenda for 17 days every March, offering a distinctive line up of performances, performers and venues. A sampling of the South's indigenous music might be heard beneath moss-draped oaks, a newly commissioned violin concerto might delight an audience gathered in one of the city's historic churches or blues legend Buddy Guy may take the stage in an elegant theater setting. In addition to the traditional offerings of jazz, blues and classical musical, the Festival also features dance and world music performances.

The Savannah Jazz Festival and the Savannah Folk Music Festival, both held in the fall, have yet to earn the prestige enjoyed by the better-known March event, but both manage to set the city's toes to tapping. Elaborate picnics in Forsyth Park are one of the highlights of the Jazz Festival, which showcases both nationally-known performers and regional musicians. The Folk Music Festival kicks off with performances in the City Market, where some form of live music can be heard nearly every weekend throughout the year.

Musicians are not the only ones taking the stage in Savannah. The City Lights Theater Company staged its first community production in 1982; Little Theatre, Inc. of Savannah has been going strong for more than 50 years.

Without a doubt, Savannah has a special place in her heart for artists. The city is home to more than 40 galleries, as well as the Savannah College of Art and Design and one of the oldest art museums in the South. The Telfair Museum of Art, which first opened in 1886, houses a permanent collection of more than 4,500 objects from America, Europe and Asia, including an impressive array of American impressionism paintings by Childe Hassam, Frederick Frieseke and Gari Melchers as well as Ashcan School paintings by Robert Henri and George Bellows. The Telfair Museum also houses North America's largest public collection of visual art by Kahlil Gibran, the internationally-acclaimed author of the Prophet. The Jepson Center for the Arts, a 64,000-square foot addition to the museum, is set to open in the spring of 2006 and will house a collection of twentieth and twenty-first century art, including African-American art, Southern art and photography. The Jepson Center will also offer room for traveling exhibits and a hands-on gallery for children and families.

The Savannah College of Art and Design is a relative newcomer to the city's art scene. The school, often referred to as SCAD, was established to prepare students for a career in the visual and performing arts, design, the building arts and the history of art and architecture, but it has also had a dynamic impact on the cultural life of the city. In order to provide students with what they considered to be an inspiring environment, college administrators selected the historic Savannah Volunteer Guard Armory to serve as the first classroom and administration building. When the newly renovated doors of the 1892 structure opened in 1979, 71 students had signed up to cross the threshold. Today, nearly 7,000 students from all 50 states and more than 80 countries are enrolled in the fully-accredited baccalaureate and master's programs available at SCAD.

The Telfair Museum houses North America's largest public collection of visual art by Kahlil Gibran, the internationally-acclaimed author of the Prophet. Photos courtesy SCVB.

Today, nearly 7,000 students from all 50 states and more than 80 countries are enrolled in the fully-accredited baccalaureate and master's programs available at SCAD. Photo courtesy SCAD.

The college has continued to successfully blend the old and the new, adapting Savannah's historic buildings for use as classrooms, studios, libraries, computer labs and production facilities, winning awards from the Historic Savannah Foundation, the Georgia Trust for Historic Preservation, the National Trust for Historic Preservation, the American Institute of Architects and the International Downtown Association in the process. SCAD, which also prides itself on serving as a leader in the marriage of art with technology, now occupies approximately 1.5 million square feet of space in the city's historic and Victorian districts.

In the mid-1990s, two SCAD graduates with degrees in historic preservation set out to make Savannah as well known for the vitality of its contemporary art scene as for its historic buildings. It was a daunting task, requiring the revitalization of a rundown Victorian landscape that stretched for blocks between the world-famous historic district and the lovely-tree lined streets of Ardsley Park. John Deaderick and Greg Jacobs, both under thirty at the time, launched their project with the purchase of the old Starland Dairy. Today, the Starland Design District is thriving. Artists and ironsmiths are among those who have found a home in the converted dairy, which is now the focal point of a booming mixed-use development that features retail shops and cafés as well as art galleries, studios and residential space. As a result of their efforts, more than 30 new businesses sprang up in the neighborhood and more than 100 apartments were restored.

As Georgia Trend magazine noted when it named Deaderick and Jacobs to their 2003 list of the Best and Brightest Young Georgians, the success of the project was no accident, "It's the result of four years of intense conversations Deaderick and Jacobs held with locals. Their goal was to make sure every resident felt included in the process - and welcome in their own neighborhood." The city helped the project along by enacting a homestead exemption to protect longtime homeowners from steep tax hikes and by introducing programs designed to assist low-income residents interested in purchasing a home in the district.

The good life that has blossomed so promisingly in the Starland Design District isn't limited to homeowners, however. On the first Friday of every month, a crowd of young artists and their supporters flock to the gallery openings and exhibits that feature the contemporary art which Deaderick and Jacobs had hoped would prosper in the heady atmosphere of Savannah's historic squares and tree-lined streets.

Many other historic buildings in and around Savannah have found new life. The Pirates' House (1754), where seamen once drank their grog, is now popular for family dinners. The birthplace of Juliette Gordon Low (built 1819-21) is owned and operated by the Girl Scouts of the U.S.A. as a memorial to their founder. The Trustees Theater, a restored art deco-era movie theater, and the Lucas Theatre for the Arts, a movie palace built in 1927 and magnificently restored in the 1990s, provide a home for the Savannah Film Festival.

The plush seats of the Lucas Theatre may be the perfect place to spend a rainy afternoon, but much of the good life in Savannah is lived out of doors. The city features a warm subtropical climate that makes outdoor activities possible year-round. Snow is a rarity along the Georgia coast, occurring on average only once in every five years - and, even then, the area receives only a gentle dusting. Things heat up in the summer, with temperatures reaching the 90s in July and August, but mild winters, with only a handful of days dipping below freezing, more than make up for it.

The Lucas Theatre for the Arts, a movie palace built in 1927 and magnificently restored in the 1990s, provide a home for the Savannah Film Festival. Photo courtesy SCVB.

Enjoy a picturesque setting for life's special moments... a wedding in Whitefield Square, with its charming gazebo or a grand and splendid affair at the impressive Westin Hotel. Photos courtesy the Westin Hotel.

Within the city's National Landmark Historic District, 22 squares offer a wide range of activities and serve as a picturesque setting for life's special moments, from a wedding in Whitefield Square, with its charming white gazebo, to a game of basketball in Forsyth Park, the recreational hub of the downtown area. Forsyth Park features extensive playgrounds, tennis and basketball courts and grassy fields that are perfect for a game of Frisbee with the dog. The sidewalk encircling the park measures almost exactly one mile, making it a popular track for local joggers and power walkers. Further south, Daffin Park is home to additional playground areas, basketball courts and soccer fields. Grayson Stadium, located on the east side of Daffin Park, is home to minor league baseball's Savannah Sand Gnats. The stadium, where Babe Ruth once played an exhibition game, has survived a hurricane that destroyed everything but the concrete outfield wall, but it may not survive the push for a larger, more modern facility.

Grayson Stadium, located on the east side of Daffin Park, is home to minor league baseball's Savannah Sand Gnats. The stadium where Babe Ruth once played an exhibition game. Photo courtesy the Sand Gnats.

Savannah's Lowcountry vistas provide a wealth of recreational opportunities as well as a scenic backdrop for the city's six public golf courses, the more than 30 additional nearby courses and the Liberty Mutual Legends of Golf PGA Tour. Photo courtesy Westin Hotel.

Beyond the city limits, a network of tidal rivers and creeks nourish one of the richest marshland ecosystems along the eastern coast of the United States. Twice a day, the tides ebb and flow, bringing nutrients and a wide range of wildlife - from Atlantic Bottle Nose Dolphin to blue crabs - into the inshore waterways. Savannah's Lowcountry vistas provide a wealth of recreational opportunities as well as a scenic backdrop for the city's six public golf courses, the more than 30 additional nearby courses and the Liberty Mutual Legends of Golf PGA Tour.

The Intracoastal Waterway, which parallels the Atlantic Seaboard, is a boaters' paradise, offering access to Florida, the Caribbean and beyond. Offshore islands like Ossabaw, Little Tybee and Wassau, can only be accessed by boat. Their quiet beaches, populated by a host of shore birds, offer the ideal location for a picnic or a rambling walk in the sand. Skidaway Island State Park offers miles of hiking trails that wind through maritime forests, along tidal marshes and beneath a canopy of pine, live oak and magnolia trees. While on the island, a visit to The University of Georgia's Marine Science Extension's aquarium might be in order. Tybee Island has been known as "Savannah's Beach" for more than 100 years. In addition to its sandy public beaches, the island features dozens of delectable seafood restaurants and a smattering of quaint boutiques. The public pier is a popular place to visit, offering spectacular views of the Atlantic Ocean and some of the best fishing in the area.

While most locals grew up with a knowledge of Tybee Island's charms, Hollywood celebrities like Sandra Bullock, who purchased a home on the island's north end, are just now discovering how good life can be in and around Savannah. It won't take long for the city to weave her spell. With her inimitable southern style, she can easily capture another heart. Her sea breeze will beguile and charm, her exuberance will delight and her reign as the "Belle of Georgia" will continue.

Photo courtesy SCVB.

Tybee Island, a boaters' paradise, is a small barrier island located 18 miles east of Savannah. It boasts a wide 3 mile long beach with an abundance of sea oat-covered sand dunes, and is ideal for sun bathing, building sand castles and people watching. Photos courtesy SCVB.

CHAPTER SIX

Tourism

By Betty Darby

Savannah loves company. In fact, according to a 2005 study by the Savannah Area Convention and Visitors Bureau (we have the latest), we welcomed 6.8 million guests that year, and the number for subsequent years is likely to have gone up.

Why do they come by the millions? There are probably millions of variations on an answer, but chances are each of those millions of variations has a common theme: reality. Savannah's attractions are the real thing, not some manufactured, artificial project put together solely to attract tourist dollars. (Well, okay, we have the usual complement of beach souvenir stores and a restaurant that features a live alligator farm, but don't the exceptions prove the rule?) Guests can tour historic homes that once housed real families, and sometimes still do. They can walk through tree-shaded squares that were drawn up as part of the oldest planned city in the country - a plan that still draws vigorous defense almost 275 years later. And when Savannah's visitors tire of the "built environment," they can check out saltwater marshes, sandy beaches and towering oak trees that eclipse the history of things like houses and cemeteries.

Savannah welcomes millions of tourists and guests each year. With unlimited delightful attractions to offer, captivate and caress your imagination with warmth and Southern hospitality. The Historic District is famous for its charming Inns where one can relax, recharge and absorb the spectacular views.

Photo courtesy The Mulberry Inn/Hampton Inn.

This Savannah 19 century restored home has become an architectural gem of the 21st century.
Savannah has become famous for her restoration and revitalization of her valuable past.
Millions of tourists that visit Savannah are attracted by - history, architecture and nature.
Photo courtesy: JT Turner Construction.

"Welcome to Historic Savannah."
Famous for Southern hospitality and charm.
Photo curtesy: SCVB.

Laid out in a series of squares by General James E. Oglethorpe in 1733, the famous Savannah Historic District is known for its architecture. A horse drawn carriage provides a leisurely view of historic Savannah, as it pauses in the front of the Mercer house. Photos courtesy SCVB.

Savannah initially did not set out to develop its tourist potential deliberately. When restoration of its stock of historic 18th and 19th Century buildings began in the late Fifties and early Sixties, the purpose was to make these architectural gems available as homes and offices for Savannahians. Tybee Island, the beachfront community within Savannah's Chatham County, was also seen largely as a "locals" beach, with a small year-round population and lots of summer homes for Savannah's "old money" families.

Tourism began to change on at least three fronts in the 1990s. First of all, the Convention and Visitors Bureau (CVB) and the local hospitality industry it represents decided to make a concerted effort to develop the more lucrative convention and meetings side of the hospitality business. At the same time, a best-selling book (John Berendt's Midnight in the Garden of Good and Evil), that painted a quirky picture of the city, inspired readers and fans to come calling. Simultaneously, real estate prices on Tybee Island began the meteoric rise that's still in progress today, as if someone just noticed that the island was largely waterfront property, and the same thing happened with historic property downtown.

Let's examine the convention and meetings development first. To bring in larger groups, the city needed somewhere to put them and a way to get them here. The Savannah Civic Center was already showing its age as a meetings site, and the Savannah airport had a limited supply of the nonstop flights that conventioneers would expect before deciding to attend a Savannah meeting.

To make the proposal work, a delicate balancing act was called for. The Savannah/Hilton Head International Airport had to recruit more airlines and persuade them to offer nonstop flights to more cities or else meeting planners wouldn't consider the city as a convention site. The convention center had be self-supporting and had to have a hotel adjacent to it in order to attract conventioneers. The luxury hotel required assurances that the convention center would be built in order to provide the guests it required.

Savannah's airport relocated to its new terminal in 1994, which placed it in an enviable position. Travelers found it small enough to avoid the hassles of major metropolitan airports, yet big enough to offer a wide range of services and flights. The trick was to convince more airlines to serve the airport, and to do so with more non-stops to major hub cities.

Today, the airport is served by nine airlines that travel to 16 different destinations, including Chicago, both New York airports, Newark, both Washington D.C. airports and, of course, Atlanta. Helping in this expansion of service has been the introduction of smaller jets to serve regional routes.

Savannah's airport got a chance to try out its international ambitions in 1996, when the city was chosen to serve as the venue for yachting events in the Atlanta Olympics. Yachting didn't attract hordes of spectators, but there were large contingents of athletes and support personnel to move in and out in a tight timeframe.

With the transportation piece of the puzzle more or less in place, attention turned to facilities. Hutchinson Island was chosen as the site for the Savannah International Trade and Convention Center and the Westin Hotel that would stand beside it.

Hutchinson Island lies in the middle of the Savannah River, directly across from Savannah's River Street, this was the chosen location for the Savannah International Trade and Convention Center This modern building outfitted with the up-to-date technology, includes a total of 365,000 square feet, among which are 100,000 square feet of divisible exhibit space.

The luxurious Westin Hotel stands beside the Convention Center. Photos courtesy SCVB.

The elegant Westin Hotel offers a full 18-hole champion golf course. Photo courtesy The Westin Hotel.

Hutchinson Island lies in the middle of the Savannah River, directly across from Savannah's River Street. By choosing this site, officials tapped into unused, acreage within clear sight of the city's main tourist area. Because the largely vacant island provided plenty of space, a full 18-hole championship golf course was built to go along with the hotel. The word "island" may spook meeting planners who want easy access to the facility, but a bridge and a fleet of newly developed passenger ferries connect the island to the mainland and remedy logistical problems.

The public center point of the island development is the trade center; a modern building outfitted with all the up-to-date technology that is essential in such a facility. That includes a total of 365,000 square feet, among which are 100,000 square feet of divisible exhibit space. Catering, a ballroom with commanding views, an auditorium with translation facilities - it's outfitted with all the amenities.

Talmaldge Bridge, named for one of Georgia's most powerful senators, connects Savannah with South Carolina. The bridge spans the Savannah River and, along with a fleet of newly developed passenger ferries, makes Hutchinson Island easily accessible. Photos courtesy SCVB & Westin Hotel.

Alongside it rises the Westin Savannah Harbor Golf Resort and Spa. With 16 floors and 403 rooms, the Westin is a luxurious hotel that sports a full array of resort aspects - which is unusual to find in a new property built almost in the shadow of a city skyline. There's the golf course, designed by Robert Cupp and Sam Snead, now home to the Liberty Mutual Legends of Golf tournament each spring. Resort facilities also include an extensive tennis complex. Here, too, you'll find the Greenbrier Spa - the only sister spa to the famous Greenbrier in White Sulfur Springs, WV. CSX, the railroad-based corporation that owns the original Greenbrier, was among the major landowners on Hutchinson Island during its redevelopment - a definite factor in the Savannah facility being able to tap into the Greenbrier mystique. These newest cards in the convention deck don't represent Savannah's full hand, of course. There were already three "convention-

sized" hotels on the mainland side, scattered along the riverfront and in the heart of the Historic District. In fact, the stock of downtown hotel rooms continues to grow, with everything from a repurposed soft drink bottling plant (an early entry in the field now known as the elegant and charming Mulberry Inn) to revitalized vintage hotels to new construction designed to blend in seamlessly with the historic setting.

Because the size of even the largest of Savannah's hotels tops out at 400 rooms, the competitive business of courting convention business has acquired an oddly cooperative attitude here. No single hotel is big enough to swallow a really major convention audience whole. Under the leadership of the Savannah Area Convention and Visitors Bureau, the major hotels cooperate and coordinate such things as reservations and transportation arrangements in the compact downtown area.

In the heart of the Historic District you will find the award-winning elegant and charming Mulberry Inn. Each day between 4:00 and 6:00 p.m. the lobby hosts the ever-popular Afternoon Tea, at which guests nibble on desserts and sip from a wide variety of teas and coffees while listening to a live pianist. Photo courtesy the Mulberry Inn.

The judicious development of public resources and the paired cultivation of private ones has opened a beautiful city up to a far wider range of meetings and conventions. Five years after the opening of its new convention center, Savannah has earned the reputation of an able host as well as a fresh and unique entry in the well-worn convention circuit.

The city's convention capabilities got a trial by fire in 2004, when Savannah had a major role in hosting the G-8 Summit, an annual gathering of world leaders from the most industrialized nations. The actual summit was 90 miles further down the Georgia coast on secluded Sea Island, but support staff and the international press corps were based at the convention center and area hotels. Even college

The city's convention capabilities got a trial by fire in 2004, when Savannah had a major role in hosting the G-8 Summit, an annual gathering of world leaders from the most industrialized nations. Photo courtesy SCVB.

dormitories, vacant during summer break, were pressed into service to house the enormous security contingent the event called for. The convention center proved it could handle such challenges as a presidential press conference and several hundred journalists who didn't necessarily speak English, and Savannah got its share of national and international exposure.

Don't let the boom in convention facilities mislead you into thinking all tourists in Savannah are wearing name badges reading "Hello! my name is..." No, while conventions are the newest segment of the hospitality industry to be courted, the everyday leisure traveler and vacationer is the most common visitor to the city.

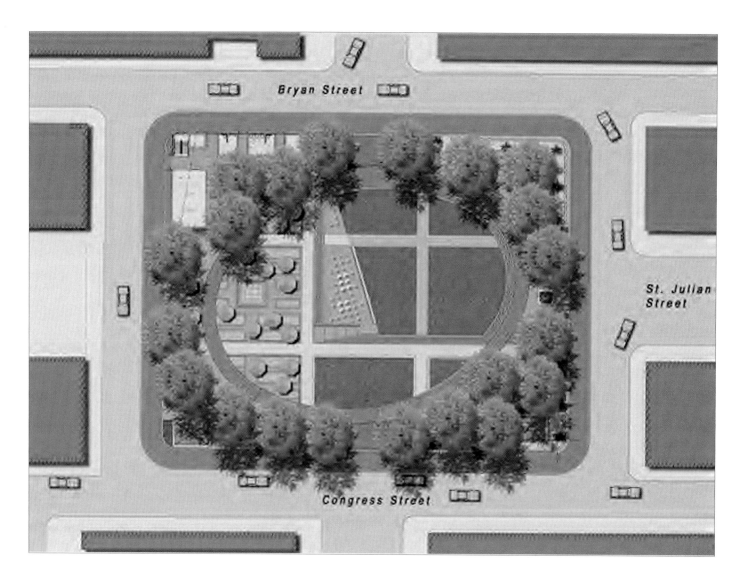

Renderings of Ellis Square when completed, sometime in late 2007, the project will feature 46 condominiums riding atop restaurant and retail space; a luxury hotel, and 25,000 square feet of office space. Some of the 1,000-plus parking spaces will be dedicated to the private sector, while others will be devoted to the public, thanks to a $25 million public investment. Photos courtesy Brooks Stillwell.

And what draws these visitors? Savannah itself - history, architecture and nature all rolled together in a very livable, walkable city. You stroll through the heart of the city's business district under a canopy of oaks, you watch young families spill out of restored Eighteenth and Nineteenth century homes, you glimpse hidden gardens behind ornate wrought iron gates and you wonder: how is all this still here, here in a working, growing city? Ah, thereby hangs a tale, as they say. And like all good tales, it has some scary parts, some close escapes, some heroes tackling heavy odds and finally, a happy ending.

Savannah is built to a plan laid out by the founder of the colony of Georgia, Gen. James Edward Oglethorpe. Central to that plan is a series of squares, 24 in all, that provide open space throughout the city. Twenty-one of them remain, with two of them mutilated by expansion projects. The other square, Ellis, once housed Savannah's old City Market, a collection of old-fashioned open-air produce and butcher stalls. That square was demolished in the 1950s to make way for a multi-level parking garage. Now, 50 years later, the City of Savannah has partnered with private investors to raze the parking garage and reinstate the square.

The finished development will result in considerably more than just restoring a rectangle of grass and trees. When completed, sometime in late 2007, the project will feature 46 condominiums riding atop restaurant and retail space; a luxury hotel, and 25,000 square feet of office space. Some of the 1,000-plus parking spaces will be dedicated to the private sector, while others will be devoted to the public, thanks to a $25 million public investment.

All of this keys off a dense footprint of land anchored by the original square and then expanding outward to incorporate adjacent buildings and former parking lots. These include the historic buildings that once housed the Savannah Morning News for more than a century. The newspaper has relocated to more convenient modern quarters, but its memory remains downtown due to the name of the new complex being: News Place on Ellis Square.

The News Place on Ellis Square will also perform another service for the city - it will help link the pedestrian route from the City Market tourist area of thriving shops and nightspots more directly to the city's bustling and original tourist area, River Street. (More on these hot spots later in these articles.)

Just after the original market at Ellis Square was destroyed, plans were announced to tear down the Davenport House to make way for a funeral home parking lot. The circa-1820 mansion had fallen on hard times and was in use as a tenement. A group of civic-minded ladies, galvanized to action by the loss of the City Market and the threat to the Davenport House, banded together and bought the structure to save it. That group was the seed from which the Historic Savannah Foundation has grown.

Today, visitors can tour the Davenport house and see how Isaiah Davenport, a prominent builder of his day, used the family home as a showcase for his talents, demonstrating things like wedding-cake plaster molding. Old Isaiah had both a large family and a keen appreciation for a budget: after touring the splendid public downstairs rooms, today's tourists can visit the far plainer quarters for the family upstairs!

The Historic Savannah Foundation, or HSF as it is better known, certainly didn't stop with the Davenport House. It stepped in repeatedly to save old buildings from the wrecking ball, buying and holding them until restoration-minded owners could be found. It was also the driving force behind local regulations that make it hard to tear down an historic structure or to build new buildings that clash too greatly with the Historic District's atmosphere. The preservation's track record is remarkable. As early as 1966, the restored downtown area earned the designation of National Historic Landmark District, one of the largest in the country.

Not all the work was done by HSF. Private homeowners, armed with low-interest restoration loans that were readily available during the 1970s, did much to bring the neglected downtown area back to its former grandeur. And as the buildings became beautiful again, instead of "bombed out" shells, tourists came to look at them, to tour the many house museums that had opened up, and to visit the private homes that opened their doors for home and garden tours each year.

The birthplace of Juliette Gordon Low was built in 1821. The house has been elegantly restored to reflect the 1880s and is furnished with many original Gordon family pieces, including artwork by Juliette Gordon Low.

This beautiful portrait by artist Albert Jonniau of Juliette Gordon Low, the founder of the Girl Scouts on March 12, 1912. Photos courtesy Juliette Gordon Low Birthplace.

Photo courtesy Juliette Gordon Low Birthplace.

Savannah is known as the walking city. Stroll under a canopy of oaks draped with garlands of spanish moss and enjoy what Savannah has to offer, Factors Walk with its string of quaint gift shops these buildings served as cotton exchanges and warehouses, or take a guided tour around a historic home, or a leisurely ride by horse and carriage and discover magic, charm and Southern hospitality at its best. Hoards of tourist visit Savannah to celebrate St. Pats day each March, that's when Forsyth Park fountain turns green. Photos courtesy SCVB.

Photo courtesy SCVB.

Savannah's historic River Street warehouses are now repurposed as nightclubs, bars, restaurants, shops and inns. They offer food and drink aplenty - stock up on atmosphere as well as food in the Boar's Head, chow down on local seafood at the Shrimp Factory, absorb Guinness and Irish folk singing at Kevin Barry's, an Irish pub. Photo courtesy The Shrimp Factory.

That's where tourism stood in the 1980s - a thriving enough business sector to include such amenities as horse-drawn carriages for tours and a sprinkling of bed-and-breakfasts to add a touch of romance to accommodations. But it was in the next decade that tourism really boomed - and one school of thought puts it down to a best-selling book that chronicles some of Savannah's scandals.

John Berendt's Midnight in the Garden of Good and Evil painted a picture of Savannah as eccentric, mysterious and appealing, with a steamy undercurrent. The book made the bestseller lists literally for years, and people not only read it, they wanted to experience it. Visitors came here in search of Midnight, and the hospitality industry obliged. Specialized tours covering sites mentioned in what was known locally as "the Book" sprang up. Souvenir shops whose stock was almost exclusively themed to "the Book" appeared. The uproar was even sufficient to hound a statue out of an historic graveyard: the enigmatic little figure that appears in Midnight's cover photo was removed from Bonaventure Cemetery and placed in the Telfair Museum for safekeeping because eager tourists were trampling graves to get their photo made beside it.

The furor has died down by now, but you'll still see vestiges of it. "The Book" tours are still offered, as are the souvenirs. Now that the attention has peaked and ebbed away somewhat, you can even tour the private home, the Mercer House, which figures so prominently in Berendt's book.

The shipping trade was the life's-blood of old Savannah. With the development of modern new facilities further upriver, the ports have moved a bit further away from the city. But the historic warehouses and streets paved with ballast stones from old sailing ships now have a new role. Savannah's River Street has become a hub for tourism. Rousakis Plaza, named for the long-time mayor who was in office during the most active period of restoration, allows guests to stroll along one of the busiest commercial rivers in the country. And, just as the water runs along one side of River Street, the old maritime buildings rise along the other. They are now repurposed as nightclubs, bars, restaurants, shops and inns. They offer food and drink aplenty - stock up on atmosphere as well as food in the Boar's Head, chow down on local seafood at the Shrimp Factory, absorb Guinness and Irish folk singing at Kevin Barry's, an Irish pub. Your shopping finds along River Street will range from tourist-tacky souvenirs to fine art and high fashion. And don't forget Savannah pralines, sinfully good confections of sugar, butter, cream and pecans, which are for sale in at least two made-on-the-premises riverfront shops. Some of Savannah's best eating, however, doesn't involve a river view - but it does involve a possible brush with a celebrity and a chance to indulge in the caloric, slow-cooked Southern heritage dishes that no one's mother has time to cook any more. We're speaking here of Mrs. Wilkes Boarding House, a legendary Savannah eatery with a history stretching back more than 60 years, and The Lady and Sons Restaurant, "ground zero" for Food Network celebrity chef Paula Deen (and sons, of course.)

Savannah is a city best seen on foot, and after all that eating, you should walk anyway. Your feet can take you to the oldest art museum in the Southeast, the Telfair Museum of Art, and standing nearby, its modern annex, the Jepson Center for the Arts. You can walk through the Ships of the Sea Museum, a salute to maritime history in general and Savannah's maritime history in particular, housed in an historic building that was once a private mansion and later a segregated school for black children. A walking trip will take you by the first African-American churches built in this country. Walk though Georgia's oldest school still in use, now a history teaching resource. And when you've worn out your shoe leather walking through Savannah's 250-plus year history, you can turn your feet to the large and diverse collection of shops and restaurants that Savannah's booming hospitality industry has made possible.

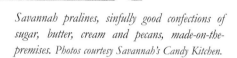

Savannah pralines, sinfully good confections of sugar, butter, cream and pecans, made-on-the-premises. Photos courtesy Savannah's Candy Kitchen.

FREIGHT
ZONE

COMMERCIAL
PERMIT
REQUIRED

Hop on board and take a leisurely tour of Savannah... experience the heart of the Historic District where you will see many elegant homes, churches, and gardens, and hear a variety of legendary tales. Photo courtesy SCVB.

First Baptist Church was granted a perpetual charter in 1801 by Governor Josiah Tattnal, Jr. Photo courtesy SCVB.

Beautiful Temple Mickve Israel - Georgia's Oldest Jewish congregation began with a group of mostly Spanish-Portuguese Jews. It is the only Gothic Revival Synagogue in the United States. Photo courtesy SCVB.

First African Baptist Church, the congregation was formed in 1788, and is the oldest African-American congregation in the United States. Photo courtesy SCVB.

The magnificent Cathedral of St. John the Baptist, this congregation was organized in 1799, and is the oldest Roman Catholic Church in Georgia. Photo courtesy SCVB.

Cemetery-Laural Grove where guided tours of fallen heroes take place
along with some scary tales and peaceful endeavors. Photo courtesy SCVB.

Bonaventure Cemetery where tomb stones are draped in hanging foliage,
and guided tours will take you on a ghostly adventure.
Photo courtesy SCVB.

Strike out from Tybee island via kayak or canoe to explore waterways through the marshes. Photo courtesy SCVB.

You'll want your car, however, when you visit Fort Pulaski National Monument, as it is halfway to the beach. Examine the elaborate fort that fell as the first victim to the accuracy of rifled cannon, demonstrating how advancing weapons technology drove the Civil War. You'll also want to check out Fort Jackson, where the Coastal Heritage Society stages reenactments.

Savannah has even joined the off-shore casino business. Several earlier incarnations of the casino ship - which involves a local dock where guests load up for the trip to international waters, where gambling is allowed - didn't prosper, but the latest venture seems to have hit the jackpot. The ship loads up for its nightly date with Lady Luck at facilities on Wilmington Island, just off Highway 80 halfway between Savannah and the beaches of Tybee Island.

No overview of tourism in Savannah would be complete without mentioning eco-tourism. Tybee Island's beaches offer the typical beach pleasures of sun, sand and rental floats, but if you want a wilder experience, you can strike out from the island (or other launching points in Chatham County) via kayak or canoe to explore waterways through the marshes. The old railroad track that once took day-trippers from Savannah to Tybee's beaches has been converted to a hiking trail. Boating is available in forms ranging from jet skis to sails. Even if you aren't bold or experienced enough to strike out on your own, tour boats are available that will take you in search of dolphins and bald eagles and other area wildlife.

Speaking of wildlife, you can get close-up looks at several facilities. Don't look for elaborate attraction aquariums or destination zoos here, but Savannah does have animal adventures to offer. Oatland Island Education Center, a unit of the Savannah-Chatham County Public Schools, is open to the public and features many habitat exhibits of native or once-native animals for the region. Look here for your alligator if you missed spotting one on the golf course! The University of Georgia Marine Extension Service operates an aquarium at its Skidaway Island facility, where you can see what you're sharing the ocean with when you go swimming in these parts. Finally, the Tybee Island Marine Science Center - while a small and humble facility - does offer such attractions as a touch tank for picking up live crabs and an aquarium spotlighting area turtles and fish.

The waving girl statue of Florence Martus, who greeted ships entering the harbor for 46 years.

The casino ship loads up for its nightly date with Lady Luck at facilities on Wilmington Island.

Climb to the top of Tybee Island's lighthouse it is the oldest and tallest in the state of Georgia. Photos courtesy SCVB.

Tybee Island has been known as "Savannah's Beach" for more than 100 years. In addition to its sandy beaches, the island features dozens of delectable seafood restaurants and a smattering of quaint boutiques. Photo courtesy SCVB.

Savannah"S Enterprise

SAVANNAH AREA CHAMBER

The Savannah Area Chamber of Commerce celebrates its 200th year anniversary in 2006 and like its founding in 1806, the Chamber's influence and strengths are evident among Savannah's exploding business climate today. Savannah-area businesses and residents enjoy an unparalleled quality of life. In the last 200 years Savannah has changed from Georgia's best-kept secret to one of the state's fastest-growing business cities as well as one of its most popular tourist destinations in the world. In fact, the Southeastern United States is the fastest-growing region in the country and Georgia is leading the charge.

1.

2.

CELEBRATING
200 YEARS
1806-2006
SAVANNAH CHAMBER

In a study by the University of Georgia and Georgia Southern University, Savannah is the fastest-growing city in the state outside of Atlanta. Savannah's residents and visitors alike enjoy a rich historical tradition and as profiled in *Georgia Trend Magazine*, our city is a carefully preserved colonial coastal village with a hip lifestyle that attracts new residents. Through the decades, Savannah's diverse economy has consistently weathered national economic cycles. Everything from the Civil War and the Great Depression, to the effects of 9/11 and current conflicts around the world, Savannah's diversity has persevered through tough times. It has been the Chamber's continued practice of championing a "pro" business environment and a tradition of business and government cooperation that has been the Chamber's vision for its 200 years in operation. Thanks to the Savannah Area Chamber of Commerce's efforts in building a solid manufacturing, distribution, tourism, military, ports operations and retail sectors, our community has a strong business community and employment base that few other communities can match.

The prominent merchants of 19th century Savannah organized the city's first Chamber of Commerce at a meeting on December 13, 1806 at the City Exchange Building, a site now occupied by Savannah's City Hall. Organizers appointed a committee of seven to draft a constitution for the government that would become the Chamber. The committee reported back to the city's businessmen on December 30,1806 proposing 17 rules that included provisions calling for initial membership fees of five dollars; for membership to be open "only to merchants, traders, factors and insurance brokers;" and for fines for "officers refusing to serve after being elected." The rules were unanimously agreed to by the 85 "subscribers" in attendance, making the Savannah Chamber of Commerce Georgia's oldest professional organization and the 7th oldest Chamber in the United States.

Like in 1806, it has been the Chamber's leadership that has paved the way for Savannah to thrive as a unified business front. Mostly a volunteer-based organization, the Chamber has benefited over the years from the expertise and influence of many of Savannah's most prominent business people, both past and present. It has been the commitments made by many Chamber volunteer leaders that have helped Savannah make its mark on the world.

The Savannah Chamber has been on the forefront of events that have shaped this community and impacted the world. Advances in business and technology made through Chamber support have reverberated throughout this community for more than 200 years. One of the most influential was the creation of a system of weights and measures in 1806 used to monitor and track shipping activity at the port of Savannah. The Savannah Chamber was on board early to the development of Savannah's shipping and port activity. The Chamber's leadership anticipated the importance that the ports would play on the growth and economic stability of Savannah.

One such port-related venture was the Savannah Chamber's backing of the 1819 maiden voyage of the *S.S. Savannah*, the first steamship to cross the Atlantic Ocean. In only 29 days, the *S.S. Savannah* arrived in Liverpool England and the Port of Savannah appeared on the world's shipping stage. In 1945, the Chamber created the Industry Committee, which was later absorbed into the Georgia Ports Authority (GPA). Today, the GPA operations, together with private sector port-related operations, account for more than 295,006 jobs statewide, billions of dollars in revenue, and income exceeding $10.8 billion annually.

The Chamber also supported another critical transportation pipeline for the bustling port city, the Central of Georgia Railroad in 1841. After a feasibility study was completed by the Chamber in 1843, 190 miles of track were laid making the Central of Georgia the longest privately-owned railroad in the country. The Central of Georgia operated for more than 136 years transporting both area-grown products like cotton, pulp and passengers to and from the farming areas of central Georgia. The last train passed through the station in 1971. The old Central of Georgia Train Station now houses the Visitor Information Center where many of the 6.9 million visitors to Savannah pass though the station each year.

In the early 1920s, the Savannah Chamber created the Savannah Port Authority, which now exists as the Savannah Economic Development Authority (SEDA). This entity was created to improve the standard of living for Chatham County residents by stimulating economic growth through the attraction of new business to Savannah. Today, SEDA provides professional site services and eases access to state and local resources. The organization, twice ranked as one of the best development groups in the country, has a clear record of success. Among SEDA's major accomplishments is the nationally-acclaimed Crossroads Business Park, home to more than five million square feet of industrial space, headquarters operations and educational institutions. SEDA also master-planned the adjacent Technology and Engineering Campus to accommodate one million square feet of class A office space, now anchored by Georgia Tech Savannah and its nationally-ranked School of Engineering.

Not only has the Chamber worked to better business for Savannah, but the organization has been instrumental in the development of community infrastructure to improve quality of life for its citizens. In the 1940s, the Chamber was successful in projects like getting Savannah's President Street extension, a road connecting Savannah's business district to outlying neighborhoods, while at the same time lobbying the city to develop a public landfill. The Chamber also contracted national suppliers to bring natural gas into the community as a power option for industrial and domestic use. All in efforts to make business and life better in this charming town by the sea.

Today, the Chamber serves more than 2,200 member businesses and strives to enhance the diverse economy of Savannah. Savannah's economy forms a strong business and employment base ranging from manufacturing to distribution, from tourism to military, from healthcare to port operations and from retail to education.

3.

1. *Savannah Chamber and the Better Business Bureau Annual Meeting in 1936 at the Savannah DeSoto Hotel.*
2. *The Citizens and Southern National Bank in 1920 at their 22 Bull Street location which was later home to Nations Bank and now home to Bank of America.*
3. *A prosperous Savannah business in 1920s.*

Through the development of community improvement councils like the Chamber's, Workforce Development Council, the Military Affairs Council and the Chamber's largest and most influential entity, the Savannah Area Convention and Visitors Bureau, the Chamber's mission is to provide quality customer service and programs that meet the needs of our members, improve the economic environment of our community, and to build a legacy of leadership for the next century.

While making business better in Savannah has always been a goal of the Chamber, creating a better workforce was the natural progression in keeping up with the demands of Savannah's growing economy. Since its founding, the Chamber has seen the connection between community and education. Working with government, educators, students and the business community, the Chamber has had a lasting impact on education in Savannah. In 1929, the Savannah Chamber engaged the Savannah Board of Public Education in discussions surrounding the need for a better trained workforce to support the growing industrial economy of coastal Georgia. That same year the Savannah Board of Public Education, in cooperation with Savannah's business community, opened the Opportunity School on Wright Square at Bull Street. The Opportunity School, now Savannah Technical College, was the first technical education school established to train young men with the skills necessary to work in Savannah's new industrial age. Today, the Savannah Technical College has more than 4,000 students and 50 programs of study centered on the technical and industrial needs of our community's workforce.

In 1935, the Chamber pushed to create more educational opportunities for its leaders of the future. By working with the Mayor and Alderman of the City of Savannah, Armstrong Junior College was founded to enhance higher educational opportunities in the community. Today Armstrong Atlantic State University has more than 7,000 students and many undergraduate and graduate degrees of study available to students' worldwide.

Savannah is a burgeoning center for technology advancements.

As Savannah flourishes with an assorted economy, our need for a trained workforce increases. The Chamber has been dedicated with providing Savannah with a workforce that is educated and trained. In 1997, the Workforce Development Council was formed to diligently work with the Savannah-Chatham School Board Council to make sure citizens have opportunities to develop necessary skills. The Chamber works as a catalyst for the development of world-class jobs and a world-class workforce in Savannah. The Chamber is taking a leadership role in facilitating the development of a workforce that matches employer needs and working with key business, education, government, and neighborhood organization leaders involved in workforce development initiatives

With Savannah growing during the new industrial age, the Chamber worked to create forums to support local government. The early 1900s became known as the Progressive Era for the Chamber when there was a move by its leadership to be more civic-minded. This is when community cleanliness and municipal services became more of a focus and this was also the time the Chamber recommended a new City Manager/Alderman form of government. The City of Savannah adopted the City Manager/Alderman based government in 1917 which is still in effect today. The establishment of the annual Savannah-Chatham Day at the Capitol resulted from the Chamber's efforts in 1967 to promote the city to the entire state. Savannah-Chatham Day is still an annual event hosted by the Chamber and attended by more than 1,000 members and state legislators.

Savannah is home to Hunter Army Airfield and Fort Stewart military bases. The two bases combined to employ more than 42,000 people and generate an annual direct federal expenditure of $1.4 billion dollars. We support our military through various councils. In 1951, the Chamber lobbied for military presence within the community. Chatham Field, which is now Hunter Army Airfield, was developed and the Chamber pushed for permanent military housing on the base.

4

The Chamber's Governmental Affairs Council (GAC) works as a voice for our member business to have their issues heard at the local, state and federal governmental levels. The GAC polls members to select priority business issues and conveys them to the appropriate levels of government. It also keeps members updated and alerts members to opportunities for individual advocacy.

While the military and the Port of Savannah are strong economic engines, the city is perhaps best known regionally and nationally as a strong tourism market. The Chamber and the Convention and Visitors Bureau (CVB) have partnered to help market and promote area businesses to potential customers all over the world. In fact, the Chamber established the CVB in 1976 as part of its effort to solicit conventions and to work on behalf of tourism, and by all measures, their efforts have been successful.

5

One of the Chamber's top priorities is to preserve and enhance the military's value in the community. With the help of the Military Affairs Council and community leadership, the Chamber has been able to accomplish this and encourage and strengthen the community's awareness and involvement. The Military Affairs Council was instrumental in protecting Savannah's area bases. Base Realignment and Closure (BRAC) took place in 2005 and was a program designed to determine which installations should be closed, reduced in size or expanded. Along with all U.S. bases, Fort Stewart and Hunter Army Airfield were subject to this critical evaluation and became a priority of the Military Affairs Council. The Chamber was instrumental in protecting our bases from the BRAC process, which ensured that the $2.2 billion economic impact area bases contribute to Savannah's economy remained intact.

4. The Port of Savannah is the nation's 5th largest container port in the United States, moving more than 16 million tons of cargo a year.
5. Savannah, founded in 1733 on the banks of the Savannah River, is a thriving commercial port and tourist destination.
6. Savannah Art Scene: The arts have always been an important element to Savannah.

In 2005, more than 6.9 million travelers spent $1.47 billion in Savannah, which generated $132 million in-state and local taxes and $151 million in federal taxes. The number of visitors at the River Street and MLK Visitor Information Centers exceeded 2 million for the first time ever. The previous record at the center was 1.8 million in 2000. Direct travel and tourism supported 20,404 jobs during the year, which accounted for 13.5% of all jobs in the area. The City of Savannah's government has also committed to the Chamber and the CVB by enlisting the help of the organization to serve as the official destination marketing firm for Savannah tourism.

The true story behind our Chamber's longevity and success can be attributed to the history of great leadership and volunteers and the extensive list of local businesses that have invested in our Chamber for decades. Savannah's ability to adapt to the changes in the business climate is a testament to the progressive attitude the Chamber has put forth since 1806. It is thanks to the members of the Savannah Chamber and their belief in community that has kept this organization going strong these 200 years; and will continue to help us build a legacy of leadership for the 200 years to follow.

6

SEDA's Vision Is Savannah's Future

"The best way to predict the future is to create it." - Peter Drucker

The new SEDA building at Savannah Harbor on Hutchinson Island opened in September 2006.

The Savannah Economic Development Authority is constantly assessing the business and economic landscape, adjusting to meet the demands of the future and developing new ways to capitalize on the region's unique assets. Twice ranked as one of the best development groups in the country, the Savannah Economic Development Authority (SEDA) stimulates economic growth through the attraction of new investment, the creation of new jobs and the support of established businesses already in the area.

Providing professional site location services with access to state and local resources, the organization has a clear record of success. Among SEDA's major accomplishments is the nationally acclaimed Crossroads Business Park, an award-winning business park with first of its kind environmental permitting and

SEDA President, Eric R. Winger.

home to more than five million square feet of industrial space, headquarters operations, and educational institutions. SEDA also master-planned the adjacent Technology and Engineering Campus to accommodate one million square feet of class A office space, now anchored by Georgia Tech Savannah and its nationally ranked School of Engineering.

SEDA was created as the Savannah Port Authority (SPA) by an act of the

Georgia Legislature in 1925. An important first step towards the rebirth of the port and the city after the demise of the cotton industry, SPA was given the power to issue industrial revenue bonds and the charge to revitalize Savannah's port industries.

Later, in 1945, Savannah's economic recovery was further fueled by the Georgia General Assembly's creation of the Georgia Ports Authority (GPA) to develop, manage and grow all of Georgia's ports. And SPA, while often collaborating with the GPA, began to concentrate on industrial recruitment more specifically.

By the mid-1980's, SPA had become an aggressive economic development force. As it gained momentum, the organization was aptly renamed the Savannah Economic Development Authority. By 1990, the organization was named one of the top ten development groups in the nation by Conway Data's Site Selection magazine, a distinction the group would achieve again in 1998.

SEDA's landmark investment in the early 1990's in the development of Crossroad Business Center was the genesis of the economic development plan to establish Savannah as an important center for warehousing and distribution. Crossroads became a gateway for dramatic growth in Chatham County and in 2006,

Gulfstream announced a $300 million expansion in 2006.

Savannah is a great place to live well.... and prosper.

the park is home to 18 companies, employing more than 2,500 area residents.

SEDA continues to actively promote the growth of port related industry while also reaching out to other traditional sectors such as manufacturing, assembly, back office operations and headquarters facilities. At the same time, with a vigilant eye on the future, SEDA has been strategically aligning the community's resources with those required by creative and technical businesses. SEDA's focus on this sector promises to sustain Savannah's dynamic economic growth well into the 21st century while increasing Savannah's per capita income by attracting higher wage jobs.

Point in case, SEDA developed the Technology and Engineering Campus with

in the Crossroads Business Center on prime property along I-95 and then donated a significant portion of it to the Board of Regents to create the Georgia Tech Savannah campus. In addition, SEDA created a team of partners to attract and retain new businesses to the area, not the east of which includes: The Creative lCoast Initiative (TCCi) - a collaboration among SEDA, the city, and county designed to market the area as a center for creativity and technology that supports 400 existing knowledge-based businesses; he Business Retention Action Team (BRAT) - a diverse team of local business twith established area businesses to help facilitate their operations and growth as well as to recruit new businesses; and the Coastal Business, Education and Technology Alliance (C-BETA) - designed to provide support and networking opportunities for knowledge-based businesses.

SEDA is essentially a marketing and sales organization, and its goal is to expand the perception of the community

beyond the traditional. While many people now know Savannah to be a great tourism destination and recognize it as a major port city, many do not realize the city's creative and technical assets -- that it boasts 14 institutions of higher education with more than 44,000 students within an hour's drive or that underneath the cobblestones streets lies 38,000 miles of fiber optic cable, just to start.

To this end, in 2004, SEDA initiated a new, aggressive marketing campaign, entitled "Live Well & Prosper." Designed to showcase Savannah's business advantages, exceptional location, business climate and infrastructure while dispelling misconceptions, the campaign promotes the region as ideal for technical and creative businesses as well as manufacturing and port-related industries.

And, it's no wonder SEDA has built its own headquarters in the middle of SEDA-owned property at Savannah Harbor on Hutchinson Island. Located just across the river from the heart of the city, SEDA fully expects the location of the 40,000 square-foot office building to further drive quality development on this urban island.

SEDA embraces Savannah's reputation as a unique, charming and beautiful city, but also emphasizes that it's "not just another pretty face" by highlighting the city's long history as a center of commerce and trade - a place where business and pleasure have been mixing well for nearly 300 years.

JCB announced the decision to locate their North American headquarters and manufacturing facility in Savannah in 1998.

Hallmark Homes of Savannah

Building on a foundation of strength

Every year, tourists from around the world succumb to the allure of Savannah's warm hospitality and irresistible architecture. Graceful homes have stood the test of time and, after being lovingly restored, have opened their doors to the public. Other historic structures have found new life as offices and shops. Each illustrates the city's rich history and inspires new generations.

Those fortunate enough to call Savannah home celebrate the city's architectural heritage in their own way. The area's leaders in new home construction, Hallmark Homes of Savannah and Jerry C. Wardlaw Construction, believe the quality and style which shaped the city's past can provide the cornerstone for a vibrant future.

Jerry C. Wardlaw Construction and Hallmark Homes of Savannah are second generation builders who have earned a reputation for excellence. Together, they have envisioned communities that offer peaceful, natural surroundings, long winding roads and country club amenities. As

partners in Landmark 24, they have opened doors to first time home buyers and honored a commitment to the fine traditions of southern living. Architectural excellence, superior craftsmanship and value are only the beginning. From the popularity of Wardlaw's affordable family homes to Hallmark's award-winning Southern Living custom homes, these builders have captured the essence of Savannah's charm and the delightful variety of its people.

Hallmark Homes

Steve, Greg and Billy Hall grew up in the home construction industry. Their father, William Hall, started Bouy and Hall Homes in 1958. As teenagers, Hall's three sons worked along side their father, learning every aspect of the custom homebuilding process from a hands-on perspective. In 1983, the brothers founded their own

company, Hallmark Homes of Savannah, Inc. Today, Hallmark Homes of Savannah, Inc., Hallmark Homes Enterprises, Inc. and Hallmark Custom Homes, LLC make up the area's largest family of builders, offering custom and semi-custom homes from $140,000 to $4 million in nearly every popular planned community in Savannah and the nearby towns of Richmond Hill, Rincon and Pooler, Georgia.

After more than two decades of developing their talents and refining the homebuilding process, Steve and Greg Hall remain at the helm. They have successfully established themselves as leaders in the field by blending the necessary elements of each home with evocative details and inventive design that set it apart from all others and mark it as a dream fulfilled. With each individual home they build, they seek to create a one-of-a-kind masterpiece that is as unique as its owners.

At Hallmark Homes, knowledge and experience combine with fresh talent and vision to provide exceptional creativity in home design. Over the years, the company has won numerous awards and honors. In the late 1990's, Steve and Greg Hall were selected as the area's exclusive Southern Living Builders, based on quality, design reputation and stability. Today, they are two of only 100 builders nationwide who represent the magazine's prestigious Builders Board.

Jerry C. Wardlaw Construction

Jerry C. Wardlaw has more than 17 years experience as a builder and developer in the residential construction industry, specializing in new homes. As the owner of Jerry C. Wardlaw Construction, he understands what's truly important in a home. Wardlaw approaches each project as if he were building it for himself; as a result, his company has revolutionized the way new homes are built by streamlining the process and keeping a close eye on costs.

Jerry C. Wardlaw Construction takes pride in delivering quality homes at reasonable prices. From concept to completion and beyond, the company works closely with home buyers. Each phase of the project is coordinated with a team of skilled building professionals to ensure the best possible experience. Wardlaw's team also carefully inspects the work of all subcontractors to provide consistent quality.

represents the beginning of a fabulously satisfying new lifestyle and the fulfillment of a dream.

Landmark 24 Realty, Inc.

Landmark 24 Realty, formed by Hallmark Homes of Savannah and Jerry C. Wardlaw Construction in 2005, is a partnership of realtors, developers and builders who have spent generations laying a strong foundation for the vibrant life Savannah offers its residents today. Working together, they offer homes in a variety of price ranges to suit every family's needs, in a variety of locations that are both naturally beautiful and convenient.

Landmark 24 sales agents guide prospective home buyers through the intricate process of finding their dream and making what could be the largest investment of their lives. The agents are experienced, home-grown professionals, many of whom live in Landmark 24 communities. They can answer the frequently-asked questions, advise first time home buyers on all the ins and outs of the system and share valuable neighborhood insights because they know about the local schools, they're familiar with community organizations and they can recommend good veterinarians, dentists and other services close to home.

With more than 1,000 new homes constructed in the past ten years in some of Savannah's finest communities, you could say that Jerry C. Wardlaw is completely at home in his role as one of the area's leading home builders. His success reflects a true appreciation of the needs of today's homeowners, from young professionals and families with children to retired couples who look forward to less demanding yard work. A wide variety of floor plans and design features are offered; enhancements, which other builders may offer only as options, come standard. Home buyers also have a variety of community locations to choose from, featuring maintenance-free amenities, such as clubhouse, fitness center, resort style pool, playgrounds and playground equipment for children and tennis courts.

A Shared Vision

For the hard working families at Hallmark Custom Homes and Jerry C. Wardlaw Construction, leadership in Savannah's local home construction industry is a serious responsibility. In the powerful partnership represented by Landmark 24, they have teamed up to create new master planned communities that residents are proud to call home.

A Landmark 24 community is the work of local builders, people who care about quality and value in their hometown. They are committed to the environment, family safety and a secure investment in southern living. Each home is a showcase of architectural excellence, flexible design and possibilities. Each home celebrates individual choice. Each home

Summer Hill at Main Street features cottage style homes priced from the $170s. The Highlands offers a variety of neighborhoods, including Cumberland Point and Spring Lake, which features new homes from the $150s. The company's newest development is in Bluffton, South Carolina. Midpoint at New Riverside, conveniently located near the intersection of SC 170 and SC 46, will offer a variety of new homes at various price points while preserving natural open spaces.

Savannah's incomparable architectural legacy has instilled high expectations among those who call the city home and has inspired the families who make up the Landmark 24 team to exceed those expectations. With new homes coming to Somersby, Harmony and the Villages at Palmetto Point, Jack Wardlaw, vice president of Jerry C. Wardlaw Construction and the 2005 President of the Homebuilders Association of Greater Savannah says, "We have a community to meet every family's budget and to fulfill every family's dream."

Landmark 24 Communities

"Today's buyer has become much more sophisticated and demands high quality and design in construction," award-winning builder Steve Hall of Hallmark Custom Homes notes. As one of the leading forces behind the Landmark 24 partnership, Hall says he strives to create communities that deliver architectural quality along with attractive lifestyle options and country club amenities in comfortable neighborhoods that are close to good schools and fashionable shopping.

Landmark 24 master planned community put families in a prime position. The major industrial and real estate boom in Chatham, Bryan and the nearby counties of Greater Savannah ensures each home will be a sound investment for the future. Landmark 24 master planned communities are located near major economic development centers where shopping malls, office buildings, restaurants and service businesses have either been built or are under construction. Each stunning community is minutes from downtown Savannah, I-16 and I-95. Some also enjoy proximity to the Savannah/Hilton International airport.

In one of the fastest growing areas

of the Coastal Empire, communities developed by Landmark 24 include single family homes in The Villages at Godley Station, The Villages at Berwick, Chapel Park, Somersby, Harmony, Spring Lakes, Cumberland Point, and Bradley Point South. Summer Hill at Mainstreet offers country club living in a picturesque natural setting in stylish Richmond Hill. Forest Lakes is a private, gated community of estate and patio homes. The community's award-winning Model Home showcases exquisite custom features that have inspired the design of many a new dream home. More than a dozen flexible floor plans, house designs and upgrade options in this upscale community let homeowners tailor their home to their own unique needs and tastes.

Amberly at Forest Lakes offers a range of innovative multi-generational home styles designed to accommodate a variety of carefree lifestyles. Specially designed single-story patio homes feature from 1,800 to 3,300 square feet and offer greater accessibility, lower maintenance and greater privacy with dual master suites available. These unique home plans are designed with expansion in mind, so pre-planned options are available to increase floor space as a family's needs shift.

EMD Chemicals Inc.

Right at Home in Savannah

Operating 24 hours, seven days a week, the EMD facility continues to be a thriving member of Savannah's community. EMD's Savannah site has nearly 200 employees.

EMD Chemicals Inc. ("EMD") and Savannah seem to be a natural fit considering the rich history of both. As Georgia's first city, Savannah's origin dates back to the early 1700's. Similarly, EMD, as the North American specialty chemical affiliate of Merck KGaA, Darmstadt, Germany, boasts roots that can be traced back several hundred years. Merck KGaA, an international pharmaceutical and specialty chemical company, had its start in 1668 when Friedrich Jacob Merck purchased the "Angel" pharmacy in Germany. In 1827, Heinrich Emanuel Merck initiated the move into industrial production. EMD (derived from Emanuel Merck Darmstadt) is named in his honor. Today, the Merck Group represents a global organization with annual sales of more than $7 billion. With over 29,900 employees it conducts its business in 55 countries.

The Savannah facility produces mica based pigments which are used in a variety of products.

EMD's Savannah site has nearly 200 employees, houses a production plant as well as departments including Technology, Product Application & Product Design, Human Resources, Engineering & Maintenance, Quality Assurance, Cost Accounting & Purchasing, Health, Safety, Security & Environmental Protection, Quality Control, Warehousing & Management and Information Services.

Products manufactured in Savannah include EMD's Iriodin® pigment product line, which are metal oxide-coated mica flakes that are used in a variety of products, including automotive coatings, printing inks and packaging materials. These mica-based pigments are also produced specifically for cosmetic applications. Marketed under the trade names Timiron® and Colorona® they are used in numerous products such as eye shadow, lipstick and nail polish. Additionally, mica products for the Food and Pharmaceutical industries are produced under the trade name Candurin®.

Founded in the United States in 1970 (under the name EM Laboratories, Inc.), EMD together with other Merck KGaA affiliates, EMD Biosciences Inc. and EMD Crop BioScience Inc., is an international organization with 1,100 employees and revenues of approx. $400 million. The EMD group focuses on innovative specialty chemicals for pharmaceutical, biotech, cosmetic, agricultural, coatings, plastics, electronics and other industrial applications.

The EMD product portfolio consists of more than 20,000 products that are widely used in a variety of products today. They include pharmaceuticals and vitamins, separation media and reagents, laboratory supplies and electronic chemicals, liquid crystals, effect pigments, and evaporation chemicals, to name a few.

Timiron® and Colorona® are used in products such as eye shadow, lipstick and nail polish.

Savannah operations also include the production of Bismuth Oxychloride crystals which are marketed under the trade names of Biflair® and Biron®. These products are utilized in printing and cosmetic applications respectively, and offer an environmentally friendly alternative to lead containing materials.

In harmony with EMD's sensitivity to the environment and commitment to safety, the Savannah plant has embraced practices to help ensure the well-being of its employees, customers and the surrounding communities. As part of this effort, the site implemented programs that have helped it to achieve compliance with ISO (International Organization for Standardization) regulations, Responsible Care® guidelines and current Good Manufacturing Practices (cGMP) requirements.

Mica products for the Food and Pharmaceutical industries are produced under the trade name Candurin®.

ISO standardization helps to ensure quality, safety, reliability and efficiency in business by distilling the latest information and technology and making it available internationally. The Savannah plant has been ISO 9001: 2000 certified since 1995.

In addition, EMD obtained Responsible Care® certification at the end of 2005. Responsible Care® is the U.S. Chemical Industry's award-winning performance initiative that has resulted in reduced emissions of 70 percent and an employee safety record that is four times better than the average of the U.S. manufacturing sector. Responsible Care® companies improve their performance by implementing world-class

EMD's Iriodin® pigment product line, metal oxide-coated mica flakes that are used in a variety of products, including automotive coatings, printing inks & plastics.

management practices; working with independent auditors; tracking performance through environmental, health, safety and security measures and extending these best practices to business partners throughout the industry. Pursuing Responsible Care® certification meshes well with initiatives already in place in Savannah. For example, the site has instituted programs to ensure an impressive safety record as evidenced by an OSHA (Occupational Safety and Health Administration) reportable incident rate that is significantly lower than the general industry standard. Also, public access to the plant is carefully controlled and occupational health is regularly monitored.

Finally, the Savannah site of EMD also adheres to current Good Manufacturing Practice regulations (cGMP) which are utilized by pharmaceutical, medical device and food manufacturers as they produce and test products.

Operating 24 hours, seven days a week, the EMD facility continues to be a thriving member of Savannah's community- attracting talented employees, responding to customer needs and ensuring a positive impact on its surrounding areas. Nearly 50% of the employees have been with the company 10 years or more - a clear indication of its commitment to competitive compensation and career development. Employee expertise is EMD's most significant asset. The experienced associates in Savannah are the key to ensuring that EMD will continue providing customers with innovative, quality products to enhance their businesses. With a focus always on ensuring the success and well-being of all stakeholders, EMD looks forward to continuing a long tradition of supplying the technology that makes a real difference in the way people feel, look and live.

For further information about
EMD Chemicals Inc.,
110 EMD Blvd., Savannah, Ga. 31407
912-964-9050
please visit www.emdchemicals.com.

CITY OF SAVANNAH

In Savannah, Progressive Local Government Supports Technology, Growth and Innovation.

Every year, millions of tourists stroll Savannah's cobblestone streets, marveling at historic mansions, scenic squares and live oaks strung with ribbons of Spanish moss. But this gracious coastal jewel offers much more than three centuries of history and a world-class tourist experience.

Savannah is also an ideal place to do business, anchored by a progressive, forward-thinking city government which supports technology, growth and innovation. The City of Savannah partners with local businesses as well as other public entities to ensure a bright future for Georgia's First City. With a thriving port, vibrant arts scene and dynamic business culture, the city combines the best of big city living with small town charm and Southern hospitality.

Since its founding in 1733, Savannah has always been defined by its entrepreneurial spirit. The earliest experiments with growing mulberry trees to produce silk in America's thirteenth colony began in Trustees Garden in the heart of downtown Savannah. In 1819, the SS Savannah became the first steam-powered ship to cross the Atlantic Ocean.

Today, Savannah has emerged as a regional hub that is home to a wide range of companies, from industry leaders in manufacturing to cutting-edge knowledge-based businesses. City officials recognize that the key to Savannah's success lies in strategic planning for future growth. Thanks to the foresight of city leaders working in conjunction with area businesses, the boundaries which once defined Savannah have expanded in every conceivable direction.

With the development of Hutchinson Island, which is located just across the Savannah River from the city's National Landmark Historic District, residential and commercial opportunities abound just north of the downtown area. A new $600 million mixed-use development along Savannah's riverfront is extending the historic riverwalk, city squares and business opportunities to the east, while a newly-annexed portion of southwest Chatham County will be home to 25,000 new residents over the next 15 to 20 years.

When it comes to technology, Savannah leads the pack. The City of Savannah supports The Creative Coast's initiative to attract, grow and nurture knowledge-based businesses. Under the city's 250-year-old cobblestone streets lie 33,000 miles of fiber optic cable. Above ground, the city boasts an active technology and creative business community with more than 300 knowledge-based businesses thriving in the coastal region. Savannah's unmatched quality of life, from its temperate climate to its year-round cultural events, continues to attract businesses from across the country and around the world.

As part of its ongoing commitment to sharing the wealth, the City of Savannah proudly funds the Economic Development Department, which is designed to facilitate business development to benefit the local economy. Through the Savannah Entrepreneurial Center, which offers small business training workshops and business incubation support services, and the Business Development Office, which assists with small business loans, city government creates a business-friendly environment which strives to maximize the economic benefit for all of Savannah's residents.

Georgia's First City also serves as a desirable location for feature films, thanks in large part to the efforts of the City of Savannah's Film Office. This unique branch of city government works directly with producers, directors and location scouts to ensure Savannah's place on the silver screen as well as a significant economic impact for local businesses. Major movies shot in Savannah include 'Forrest Gump,' 'Midnight in the Garden of Good and Evil,' 'The Gingerbread Man' and 'The Legend of Bagger Vance.'

In the historic downtown area, exciting projects like Ellis Square define the City of Savannah's commitment to supporting the business community and improving the quality of life along the coast. This unique public/private partnership combined $37 million in public funding with $46 million in private funding to restore one of Savannah's original squares and to create a vibrant downtown destination for visitors and residents alike.

Originally designed by General James Oglethorpe in 1733, Ellis Square was razed and converted into a City Market parking garage in the 1950's. Now, Ellis Square is being brought back to life. The City of Savannah is currently building a 1,075-space underground parking garage and designing a square which remains faithful to Oglethorpe's vision while meeting the needs of twenty-first century Savannah. At the same time, private businesses are creating a world-class hotel, condominium, retail and office facility within steps of historic City Market.

However, Ellis Square is just one shining star in the city's future. Another exciting project on the horizon is the Battlefield Park Heritage Center, a first-class visitor experience devoted to three centuries of Savannah history. Located along the gateway to the city's National Landmark Historic District, Battlefield Park will feature a historically-accurate recreation of the Spring Hill Redoubt, an earthen fortification on the site of one of the bloodiest battles of the American Revolution. On October 9, 1779, an estimated 7,000 troops from three continents clashed for control of the British-held village of Savannah.

Thanks to the efforts of The Coastal Heritage Society, a local non-profit organization, and funding from the City of Savannah, the Battlefield Park Heritage Center will reconnect the Roundhouse Railroad Museum, which is the oldest and most complete antebellum railroad manufacturing and repair facility in the United States, to modern-day railroad lines, creating a multi-faceted heritage attraction. Roughly $30 million of public funds have already been earmarked to help with the project.

When it comes to business development, technology and culture, the City of Savannah serves as a critical partner in shaping the future of the region. With a strong local business community, an unmatched quality of life and an ongoing to commitment to success, the future for business in Savannah looks very bright, indeed.

•*Facing page photo top left:: Johnson Square.*

•*Facing page photo lower left: Wrights Square.*

•*Top photo this page: Chippewa.*

•*Lower photo this page: Savannah Port.*

NORTH POINT REAL ESTATE

By providing comprehensive real estate solutions that add value to clients' needs, North Point Real Estate has grown into an award-winning business comprised of four divisions -Industrial, Office, Residential, and Retail. Their innovative, solution driven approach has helped companies simplify the development process from start to finish.

North Point delivers the experience, tools, resources and relationships that give clients the ability to thrive in today's competitive marketplace. Our hands-on, client-centered approach provides companies with the ability to make informed decisions followed by efficient and effective execution of those decisions. North Point offers a wide range of corporate real estate services, from site location analysis and lease negotiations to construction and property management. North Point can proactively manage all of your real estate needs.

In addition to their development services, North Point embraces the opportunity to give back to the communities in which they work and live. Their real estate developments enhance the surrounding environments in a variety of ways - from building quality homes where families will create lasting memories to developing facilities that bring jobs to the community.

North Point's core values, which are focused around integrity, quality service, citizenship and value-added solutions, are woven into each of their four divisions.

North Point Industrial has successfully developed a variety of built-to-suit facilities, ranging from office/warehouse flex facilities to distribution centers. Many major national corporations have hired North Point Industrial for projects across the nation.

North Point Retail has a proven record of success in retail development. They have spearheaded major retail projects across the Southeast and have landed national tenants in several award-winning retail centers.

With a goal of creating communities where families love to live, North Point Residential has developed and master-planned thousands of acres of residential real estate. They offer development services ranging from land acquisition and entitlements to sales and marketing. Their local, regional and national marketing campaigns have resulted in over $400,000,000 of residential sales in Georgia, South Carolina and North Carolina.

In addition to tremendous sales success, North Point Real Estate is also deeply concerned with the natural environment. North Point Residential, for example, follows a unique master-planning process that respectfully blends natural amenities and green space. At Southbridge, North Point was able to preserve more than one-third of the land, which included pristine woodlands and lush wetlands. "We try to maximize the use of green space to create an attractive community," says Jeff Jepson, principal at North Point. "The more nature we can preserve, the more we contribute to the quality of life."

The professional team at North Point believes in pursuing innovative approaches to business development. They aim to help clients maximize the value of their real estate assets by following a thorough, creative and exhaustive approach. Whether those needs are for a small branch bank, a master-planned community or a warehouse distribution center, North Point has the experience and resources to deliver quality service with immediate results.

North Point's experienced team specializes in finding effective solutions to corporate real estate opportunities.

LIST OF SERVICES:

• **Tenant Representation**

• **Build to Suit Development**

• **Equity Placement**

• **Debt/ Financing**

• **Site Location Analysis**

• **Economic Incentives Negotiation**

• **Lease Analysis**

• **Demographic Research**

• **Lease Administration**

• **Construction Management**

• **Project Management**

• **Operating Expense Reviews**

• **Property Management**

• **Asset Management**

Our master-planned communities feature quality homes with unbelievable amenities.

Some of the challenging champion golf courses adorn our communities.

OFFICE   INDUSTRIAL   RETAIL   RESIDENTIAL

Savannah/Hilton Head International Airport

The Airport's inviting, Savannah Square area reflects the city's charms and hospitality and features rocking chairs that are always a popular resting spot for travelers to enjoy.

Whether planning for group travel or an intimate getaway for two, Savannah / Hilton Head International makes flying to and from the beautiful city of Savannah simply effortless. Among its many attributes, the airport offers eight airlines that provide 46 daily departures and nonstop connections to 16 destinations in addition to countless conveniences including covered, onsite rental car facilities, free Internet connections in the business center, a variety of restaurants and shops and a visitor center that offers maps and local tourist information. Without a doubt, Savannah / Hilton Head International provides travelers with a gracious gateway to Southern hospitality.

The history of Savannah / Hilton Head International dates back to 1918 where an area on the south side of Daffin park opened as the first landing field in Savannah. The east-west strip was approximately 2,500 feet long and 450 feet wide. Ten years later, a 730-acre tract of land off White Bluff Road was selected as the site for a modern airport to be developed jointly by the city and county. The new Savannah Airport opened on September 20, 1929 with the inauguration of air express and passenger service between New York City and Miami by Eastern Air Express.

Throughout the 1930s, the airport continued to expand service and reach new milestones beginning with a plane named the *City of Savannah,* which was the first official aircraft to operate from the airport. Just one year later, the Eastern Air Transport aircraft was christened with water from the Savannah River and served as Georgia's first intrastate airline with regular service to Atlanta via Augusta. Growth quickly "took off" and in 1932, a city resolution christened the airport Hunter Field. Just five years later, daily service began between Savannah and Gulf Coast points and then in 1941, Delta Air Lines inaugurated service from the Savannah area with two, daily roundtrips to Atlanta via Augusta.

Air travel horizons would soon expand with the first flight to the Midwest in 1945. Savannah's Mayor at that time, Peter Nugent, added true Southern flare to this momentous occasion by sending fellow Chicago Mayor, Edward J. Kelly, a bag of Dixie Crystals sugar and a package of fresh shrimp!

SAVANNAH'S AIRPORT IN 1959

1948

Air service at Savannah/Hilton Head International is provided by AirTran Airways, American Eagle, Continental Express, Delta, Delta Connection, Northwest Airlink, US Airways and United Express.

The majestic fountain statue welcomes all air travelers at the Terminal Building entrance and symbolizes the Airport's international status as she holds the world in her hands and lifts it to new heights.

Over the years, Savannah's air services continued to expand. First, the airport's location shifted from Hunter Field to Travis Field located in northwest Savannah and soon, runways had to be extended to accommodate the longer take off runs of the new generation jet aircraft. Internally, the airport was changing as well with the creation of an Airport Commission to oversee the need for ongoing expansion; a Commission that still exists to this day. In 1994, a new 275,000-square foot, $43 million terminal building opened taking air service for Savannah and surrounding areas to a whole new level. In fact, traffic from nearby Hilton Head Island increased to such an extent that in 2002, the Savannah International Airport revised its name to become Savannah / Hilton Head International.

In 2006, a $13 million terminal expansion project was launched to add five gates and an additional 6,600 square feet of concession space to the current concourse.   A new parking garage, constructed above the original short-term lot, was also part of this expansion resulting in 1,690 premium parking spaces at an estimated cost of $34 million. In addition, the new deck features a light system to direct passengers to available spaces as well as covered walkways between the second and third levels of the deck connecting it to the terminal building.

Today, Savannah / Hilton Head International is served by: AirTran Airways, American Eagle, Continental Express, Delta, Delta Connection, Northwest Airlink, US Airways and United Express. General aviation services are handled by fixed base operator Signature Flight Support, which provides fueling, maintenance, ground handling and passenger services. Piston aircraft maintenance, aircraft rentals, flight training and a variety of pilot supplies are available through Savannah Aviation. Air Cargo service is handled by DHL, FedEx, and UPS.

With its "First In Service" initiative, the airport provides travelers with superb travel convenience in addition to many "extras," making for a truly enjoyable experience. A few of those extras include restaurants such as Phillips Famous Seafood, Starbucks, Nathan's, Wolfgang Puck's, Dewar's Clubhouse, Burger King and Pizza Hut as well as a full-service salon and arcade. Passengers also enjoy Wireless Internet service, which is available throughout the terminal, the Paradies Shops and PGA Tour Shop, as well as the Passport Club, which has opened its doors to all airline club members. Most importantly, however, Savannah's charms will continue to beckon while healthy and consistent growth promise to be as integral a part of the airport's future as it has been of its past.

WSAV-TV

On February 1st, 1956, a new TV station made its debut in the Coastal Empire and Low Country. On that day, WSAV-TV was born, broadcasting NBC Television programs to an audience fascinated with the new medium.

The 1963 Miss Savannah Beauty Contest is seen live for the first time on WSAV from the new Broadcasting Center on East Victory Drive. Kurt Avery (seen on left) hosted the event.

WSAV-TV's first location was atop the old Liberty National Bank Building on Bull and Broughton in downtown Savannah, which had been the home of WSAV radio since 1939. However, the needs of the new television operation almost immediately outgrew the small studio space. Harbin Daniel, then the owner of WSAV Radio and Television, began making plans to build a new state-of-the-art broadcasting facility on historic Victory Drive.

Construction took over a year, and on the evening of Saturday, July 23rd, 1960, at 6:30pm, the inaugural broadcast took place from the new Victory Drive Broadcasting Center. The new studio was so large it was able to contain the Savannah Symphony Orchestra, WSAV talent, and dignitaries from local and state government. A new taller transmission tower and a much more powerful transmitter, built on the new site, also went into operation that night, bringing television to a much larger audience than ever before.

WSAV has experienced many milestones during its first fifty years. It was the first local station to broadcast in color, the first station to air live coverage of Savannah's St. Patrick's Day Parade, the first to receive network transmissions via satellite, the first station to have a satellite and uplink truck and a live microwave truck for local news.

WSAV Television was home to a host of popular broadcast personalities over the years, many still remembered today by longtime Savannah residents.

Kurt Avery hosted the morning show, "3 for the Show", a news-talk program very similar to today's "Coastal Sunrise". It featured interviews with a variety of guests, and frequent cooking segments using one of two fully equipped kitchens built right into the back of the WSAV studio. They were identical in every respect except that one was fueled by natural gas, and segments in that kitchen were sponsored by The Savannah Gas Company. The other was electric, with all its segments being sponsored by Savannah Electric.

Captain Sandy became a popular mainstay right from the beginning with his daily weather reports, delivered with the help of his puppet sidekick Wilbur the Weather Bird, along with Arthur Mometer, and Calamity Clam.

One of the most recognizable characters from WSAV's past is Captain Sandy and his sidekick Wilbur the Weather Bird. Captain Sandy was broadcast on WSAV beginning sign-on night, February 1st 1956 until about 1982.

The team of Chief Meteorologist Ben Smith (left) and News Anchors Tina Tyus-Shaw (center) and Russ Riesinger (right)
present WSAV News 3 "On Your Side" each weeknight at 6 and 11pm.

For almost 20 years Lyndy Brannen (left) has been waking up Savannah as a
host of WSAV's Coastal Sunrise show. He, along with Kim Gusby (center) and
Meteorologist Lee Haywood (right) have made Coastal Sunrise
one of the most popular shows on WSAV.

And there was Ralph Price, the most respected local newsman of his time. He tackled the hard issues with anyone who was anyone making news in the early days. His "Candid Opinion" interview show aired each night within the WSAV news block, which in those days was from 7-7:30pm. Ralph also anchored the 11pm news on WSAV until the early 1980's.

Through all the years, WSAV Television continued to evolve and grow, to meet the changing needs of viewers throughout the Coastal Empire and Low Country.

WSAV was purchased from the Daniel family in 1976 and has gone through several ownership changes since then. In 1997, WSAV Television came under the ownership of Richmond Virginia-based Media General, which owns a number of television stations and newspapers throughout the Southeast.

Media General believed that WSAV had significant growth potential, and beginning in 2003, significant changes were implemented. That Fall, Coastal Sunrise returned to the morning schedule, and made an immediate impact. In August of 2004, WSAV's news and marketing look was completely revamped. Sharper graphics, a state of the art news set, and a new logo were introduced around a new focus—"On Your Side." "On Your Side" means WSAV News is committed to digging deeper, asking the tough questions, and getting results for our viewers. Every day. Every newscast. This commitment has paid off, as WSAV was named Georgia's best newscast in 2006 for the second year in a row.

This news commitment, combined with the acquisition of such popular entertainment programs as Oprah, Dr. Phil, Wheel of Fortune, and Jeopardy, has helped WSAV grow significantly in audience share over the past three years.

But there is more to come. As TV technology evolves, so does WSAV.

WSAV has been making the transition from analog to digital over the last few years and is just now putting on the finishing touches. On May 9th, 2005, WSAV began broadcasting a full power digital High Definition signal to our viewers. Server-based digital video playback has taken over where video tape once reigned supreme. Crystal clear images, broadcast over satellite and displayed on large plasma screens, have replaced the snowy black and white pictures on tiny screens that people first watched on Channel 3 a half century ago.

Beginning in the fall of 2006, WSAV will not only be Savannah's NBC affiliate on its analog and primary digital channel, but it will also become the home for My TV, a brand new broadcast station that will air on WSAV's secondary digital channel.

For fifty years, WSAV Television has delivered quality programming, news and information to the people of Savannah, the Coastal Empire, and the South Carolina Low Country. Our commitment is stronger than ever, as WSAV begins its second fifty years.

Memorial Health:

World-class healthcare – right here in Savannah

Savannah is renowned for its history, beauty, and hospitality. It is also becoming renowned as a center for exceptional healthcare. Memorial Health, headquartered on a 43-acre campus on Savannah's east side, serves a 35-county area in southeast Georgia and southern South Carolina. Memorial Health University Medical Center (MHUMC), a 530-bed teaching and research hospital, is the flagship of the organization, which is also home to the region's only children's hospital, Level 1 trauma center, and Level 3 neonatal intensive care nursery. Memorial Health also offers a cancer institute, a heart and vascular institute, a rehabilitation institute, a two-state home health division, nearly 40 physician practices, a 24-hour nurse call center, and ambulance and helicopter emergency transport services.

Memorial Health strives to be the best and is recognized for its efforts. For the past three years, the organization has been named a Distinguished Hospital by J.D. Power and Associates and one of the "100 Best Companies to Work for" by *Fortune* magazine. In 2005, *Consumers Digest* rated MHUMC number 23 in its list of the nation's safest hospitals. Healthgrades, a leading provider of healthcare quality data, has awarded MHUMC five stars, its highest rating, for overall cardiac care three years in a row. *Modern Healthcare* magazine has listed Memorial Health in its "Top 100 Health Hospitals" for two years. And, for six years in a row Hospitals & Health Networks magazine has rated the medical center one of the "Most Wired" hospitals in the nation. The accolades and awards are many, however Memorial Health's mission is very simple – to help people feel better.

In pursuit of this mission, the organization consistently provides more specialists, services, and facilities to its offerings. Recently, Memorial Health reinforced its commitment to world-class cardiovascular care with a new, dedicated Heart & Vascular Institute. The 189,000-square-foot facility features state-of-the-art surgical facilities, including an endovascular suite, as well as the region's only EECP non-invasive treatment for angina, TMR laser surgery to treat cardiac pain, and biplane angiography, which enables physicians to see and treat a stroke as it occurs.

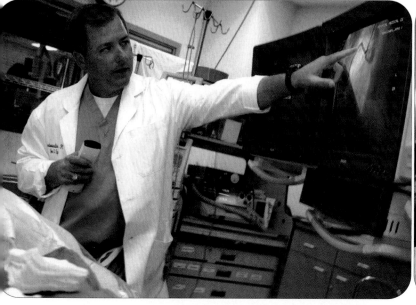

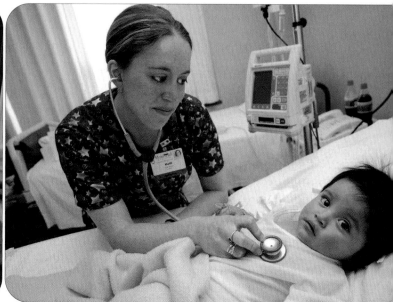

Memorial Health is also home to world-class cancer care. The Curtis and Elizabeth Anderson Cancer Institute* (ACI) at MHUMC features the region's only dedicated practices for breast care, gynecologic oncology, and pediatric oncology, as well as a genetic counseling program. Three of the ACI's physicians have been designated "Distinguished Cancer Clinicians and Scientists" by the state of Georgia. Eight multi-disciplinary, disease-specific management teams plan treatment programs for each patient; a special "nurse navigator" guides each patient through the complex process of fighting cancer. The ACI also offers support groups, educational programs, art therapy, massage, pet therapy, and an annual free weekend retreat for cancer patients and their families, treating the whole person - mind, body, and spirit - not just the disease.

The Rehabilitation Institute at MHUMC offers comprehensive inpatient and outpatient services to facilitate recovery from life-changing illnesses or accidents. From brain and spinal cord injuries to recovering from joint replacements, the Rehabilitation Institute helps people return to fulfilling lives through special programs, aquatic therapy, sports, and even fully-simulated home and shopping environments.

Recruiting from among the nation's best, Memorial Health hires only board-certified physicians. Memorial Health University Physicians (MHUP) includes primary care physicians and more than 60 specialists who concentrate on everything from orthopedics to vascular surgery to women's breast care. Memorial Health also offers primary care and specialty physicians in a variety of locations, making access to top-notch care more available than ever.

The organization's most recent project partners the ACI and the Mercer University School of Medicine in building a new cancer research center, which will be one of only a few centers in the U.S. to focus on molecular genetic cancer research. The new facility will be headed by Jeff Boyd, Ph.D, a renowned scientist formerly with Memorial Sloan Kettering in New York.

Memorial Health has been thriving in Savannah for 50 years, delivering world-class healthcare to hundreds of thousands of people. During those years, from performing the region's first open-heart surgery in 1967 to building a first-class research facility, the dedicated healthcare professionals at Memorial Health have saved lives, fought diseases, offered hope - and helped people feel better.

Photography: Russ Bryant

Disclaimer:
*The Curtis and Elizabeth Anderson Cancer Institute at Memorial Health University Medical Center is not affiliated with the University of Texas M.D. Anderson Cancer Center.

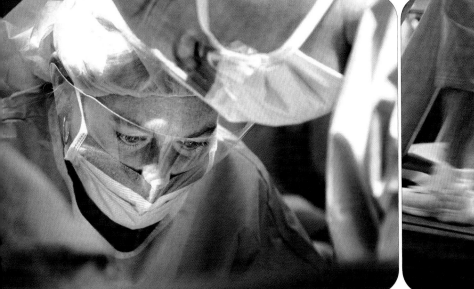

INTRODUCING GULFSTREAM AEROSPACE

Savannah, Georgia's largest manufacturer,
Gulfstream Aerospace is the world's leading maker
of business jet aircraft.. Since 1958 when it produced
its first turbo-prop corporate airplane, the
Gulfstream I, Gulfstream has produced more than
1,500 aircraft for use by Fortune-500 companies,
private citizens, the U.S. government, and foreign
governments for surveillance missions and
transporting their heads of state.

Gulfstream Aerospace

A wholly owned subsidiary of General Dynamics, Gulfstream
employs approximately 7,900 employees at seven major locations
in the U.S., Mexico and England. In Savannah, approximately
4,500 people are employed at the aircraft production, completion and
service facility adjacent to the Savannah-Hilton Head International
Airport. In addition to its primary business, Gulfstream also manages six
General Dynamics Aviation Services maintenance centers across the
United States.

Today Gulfstream offers six models of business-jet aircraft and is
comprised of many organizations spread out among various locations,
however the company traces it roots to a single airplane built by a legendary
aircraft manufacturer on Long Island, N.Y. In 1958, the first Gulfstream
aircraft was designed and produced by Grumman Aircraft in Bethpage,
N.Y. Grumman produced this turbo-prop plane until its successor, the
Gulfstream II; a jet-powered aircraft, was introduced in the mid-1960s. It
was during this time when Grumman officials decided to separate the civil
and military aircraft production lines to reduce costs.

By the mid-1970s, Grumman's business aircraft production plant in
Savannah was growing with the increasing demand for business-jet aircraft. The facility now included a service center where Gulfstream aircraft
owners could take their planes for maintenance and repairs. From the GII
design, the plant produced two NASA Space Shuttle Training Aircraft
that simulated space shuttle flights for pilot and astronaut training. The
GII holds the distinction of the first corporate/business aircraft to cross
the Atlantic Ocean nonstop.

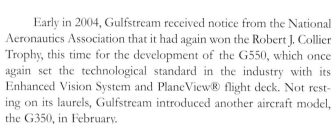

In 1978, Grumman sold its Gulfstream aircraft production and service business to Alan Paulson, an entrepreneur who owned an aircraft service and refurbishment company in California. A life-long aviation enthusiast, Paulson took the company into the next two decades by introducing two new aircraft, the Gulfstream III and long-range Gulfstream IV. (GIV). The 500th and last GIV/GIV-SP rolled off the production line in 2002, establishing it as the best-selling large-cabin aircraft ever built.

With the introduction of the ultra-long-range Gulfstream V (GV) in 1993, Gulfstream announced that for the first time, it would build two aircraft models – the GIV-SP and GV – concurrently. The GV took its first flight in 1995 and two years later, it won the aviation industry's most prestigious award, the Robert J. Collier Trophy, joining the ranks of the Apollo mission, Chuck Yeager and the Space Shuttle Program as Collier recipients.

In 1999, General Dynamics (NYSE:GD) purchased Gulfstream Aerospace, helping Gulfstream further establish itself as a supplier of special-mission government aircraft and providing General Dynamics with an aerospace division to accompany its marine, land systems and information systems and technology divisions.

By 2001, Gulfstream produced two aircraft – the GIV-SP and the GV – and was in development with the next generation GV, later named the G550. In May, when Gulfstream announced the purchase of Galaxy Aerospace and the two business-jet aircraft it produced, it doubled the number of models in its fleet overnight. Gulfstream immediately renamed the aircraft the G100 and G200. Earlier the same year, General Dynamics Aviation Services was established following the acquisition of five service centers located in Las Vegas; Dallas; Minneapolis; Westfield, Mass; and West Palm Beach, Fla.

While 2001 would forever be known as the year of acquisitions, 2002 would be known as the year of fleet expansion. In October, Gulfstream introduced a seven-aircraft fleet and new nomenclature that better described each aircraft's relative size and range. Gulfstream offered business jets ranging from the mid-cabin, high-speed G100 to the new large-cabin, ultra-long-range G550.

In 2003, Gulfstream acquired its first overseas service center in London, England; the G550 received certification by the Federal Aviation Administration; and the large-cabin, long-range G450 was introduced.

Early in 2004, Gulfstream received notice from the National Aeronautics Association that it had again won the Robert J. Collier Trophy, this time for the development of the G550, which once again set the technological standard in the industry with its Enhanced Vision System and PlaneView® flight deck. Not resting on its laurels, Gulfstream introduced another aircraft model, the G350, in February.

In 2005, the new wide-cabin, high speed G150 was rolled out; took its first flight and was certified. The G150 replaced the G100 in the market offering.

Gulfstream aircraft currently hold more than 100 city-pair speed records.

Gulfstream has been the leading business-jet manufacturer for decades. Its engineering and development teams have pushed the envelope of technology to design and build the safest, most dependable, reliable and state-of-the-art business-jet aircraft. Along with the technologically-advanced PlaneView flight deck, which incorporates Gulfstream's industry-leading Enhanced Vision System, Gulfstream designers optimize cabin layouts and hand-select materials that add even more passenger comfort. But it doesn't end once the purchase is completed; Gulfstream's highly skilled technicians and award-winning worldwide product support network ensure all of the models that comprise the Gulfstream fleet operate at the optimum level for which they were designed. It's a combination of excellence in a variety of areas – design, engineering, production, sales, service and support – that has made Gulfstream what it is today, simply the best.

In early March 2006, Gulfstream announced it was embarking on a 7-year, $300 million expansion plan for its Savannah operations. Some 1,100 new jobs will be created, thereby ensuring the company remains a major cornerstone in Savannah's economic community.

For comprehensive information on Gulfstream, please visit its Web site at www.gulfstream.com

Savannah Morning News.

World wars and peace - natural disasters - elections - assassinations. The headlines from 155 years of history scream out from the dozen framed copies of the Savannah Morning News that line the walls of its new facility in Georgia's oldest city.

SAVANNAH, GEORGIA, SATURDAY MORNING, JANUARY 28, 1854.

The journey of the Morning News, from its first edition on January 15, 1850, to its spacious and modern plant mirrors the trials and triumphs of Savannah itself. "Our platform is embraced in words, neutrality, independence and industry," wrote Editor William Tappan Thompson in that inaugural issue. "Our aim will be to give our subscribers a cheap, reliable and comprehensive newspaper, and to the business man an advertising medium through which he may reach all classes of the community. While we shall preserve our neutrality inviolate, we shall in no instance compromise our independence, and what patient industry can do to make our sheet useful and popular, shall be accomplished."

That independence was all but swept away in December of 1864 when a Union army under General William Tecumseh Sherman entered the city after completing its famed "March to the Sea." The Morning News was one of the casualties of that campaign - its editors left the city just before Sherman's arrival.

The newspaper resumed publication in January of 1865, but not as the Morning News. It was called the Daily News and Herald until September of 1868 when its banner became the "Savannah Morning News." The period is also part of the banner, a distinctive element that over the years has survived several efforts to eliminate it.

The Morning News added a distinctive writer to its staff in the 1870 when Joel Chandler Harris, the author of the "Uncle Remus" folktales, became an associate editor. Harris wrote a column and editorials until 1876 when a yellow fever epidemic struck Savannah.

•Front of the Daily Morning News, January 28, 1854.
•The first editor of the Savannah newspaper, William Tappen Thomas.
•This rocking chair belonged to Joel Chandler Harris. Today it sits in the publisher's office.

The author and his family then fled to Atlanta where he joined the staff of the Atlantic Constition. During Harris' tenure, the paper was owned by Col. John Edward Holbrook Estill, who had purchased a half-interest in the paper in 1867 and bought it entirely in 1869. Estill remained its owner until his death in 1907.

That lengthy span of influence was rivaled by Herschel V. Jenkins, who acquired the Morning News in December of 1926. In 1931, Jenkins purchased Savannah's afternoon newspaper, the Evening Press. The two newspapers staffs thereafter shared the same location, but little else as a fierce rivalry for local stories simmered for decades.

The two papers continued under Jenkins' stewardship until 1957 when he sold them to Savannah banker Mills B. Lane and Florida newspaper executive Alva Chapman.

The final sale of the Morning News and Evening Press came in 1960 when they were bought by William Shivers Morris Jr., publisher of The Augusta Chronicle and Augusta Herald. After his death in 1967, his son - William S. "Billy" Morris III - took over the company and continued to expand it. During all these changes, there was one constant for the newspaper - its location.

The original Morning News building was erected in 1850. Additions and annexes continued until the newspaper consisted of six connected buildings and took up an entire block along West Bay Street. Other physical changes included the method of producing the paper as the Morning News went from hand-cranked presses to wooden and metal type to linotype to offset presses.

Competing newspapers came and went, and the antagonism between the Morning News and the Evening Press dimmed when the two papers' editorial staffs merged in 1969. The Evening Press, first published in 1891, eventually fell victim to changing readership habits. Its last edition was on Oct. 31, 1996.

A squeeze was also being put on the Morning News: It had outgrown its Bay Street home. The six buildings contained only 78,000 square feet, necessitating the constant shifting of newsprint and pallets of preprinted advertisements.

So in October of 2004, the Morning News moved 6 miles to the west, to the fastest growing part of Chatham County. Its new home is palatial. The Savannah Morning News now has 145,000 square feet in its production facility and 75,000 square feet of occupied office space. An additional 25,000 square feet of unfinished space is available for future expansion.

"This building stands as a symbol of our commitment to this newspaper and this community and reflects the important position the Savannah Morning News holds within the Morris Communications family of enterprises," said Billy Morris, whose Augusta-based media conglomerate now includes Morris Publishing Group is a wholly owned subsidiary of Morris Communications Company LLC and publishes 26 daily, 12 nondaily and 23 free community newspapers in the United States, 27 radio stations and numerous magazine and other publications.

Morris Communications Company was careful to include reminders of the past in the new building. The framed editions are joined by a circa-1850 Washington Hand Press. Bricks, like those in Savannah's squares, line a portion of the floor, and an photograph of the oak-lined drive at Wormsloe plantation graces an entire wall.

These testimonials make it clear that the Morning News' historic past is the foundation of its future.

• *The original Morning News building in 1925.*
• *The Savannah Morning News moved to its new 245,000 square foot building in November of 2004.*

Lott + Barber Architects

Since opening their doors in 1990, Lott + Barber Architects have set their sights high,
in terms of professional design standards, community involvement, and personal client service.
As a result, they have developed not only an impressive portfolio of award-winning design
projects, but also a loyal client base representing more than 90% repeat business.

For more than 15 years, Lott + Barber Architects have provided a diverse range of services, including architecture, sustainable planning and urban design, facilities management and interior design. The firm's diverse range of clients, includes Georgia Southern University, The University of Georgia, First Chatham Bank, The Savannah Bank, Armstrong Atlantic State University, Sea Island Bank, The Lucas Theatre and St. Joseph's/Candler Health System.

Today, the sky continues to be the limit. This Savannah firm is among the first of architectural firms in the country using Building Information Modeling, an innovative three-dimensional software design program developed for the aerospace industry. The same approach being used to design the Freedom Tower at the World Trade Center site.

Building Information Modeling, or BIM as it is often called, represents a paradigm shift in design. Before now, a design resided in only one place – the mind of the architect. Through the creation of a fully integrated 3-D, data-rich model, BIM now allows that vision to be shared. Instead of explaining flat elevations and floor plans, Lott + Barber Architects can now show 3-D BIM images and videos from any perspective. What's more, the visual imagery evolves simultaneously with the building design, providing an invaluable decision making tool.

Top photo: The Armstrong Center Lobby as rendered in BIM

Lower photo: Lucas Theatre for the Arts Restored Interior

University of Georgia Forest Resourse Center, Effingham County

Lott + Barber also offers a diverse range of planning services for both public and private sector clients. Bridging the gap between horizontal master plans and vertical building design, plans developed by LBA also emphasize the importance of community, social, and natural resource considerations. For example, the master plan developed by Lott + Barber Architects for the City of Port Wentworth received critical acclaim from the American Planning Association as well as the National League of Cities. Showcasing the planning abilities of Lott + Barber Architects, the firm designed this master plan to incorporate community diversity, wetlands protection and mixed-use of commercial, office, civic and residential space. The success of this plan is evident through the resulting development of Rice Hope, a 1300 acre new urbanist community, also designed by Lott+Barber Architects.

Since Forrest R. Lott, AIA, started the business in 1990, the firm's growth has been guided by a clear focus on delivering excellent service and high-quality design to clients who demand the best. Since then, Lott + Barber Architects has been quietly producing distinctive planning and building designs across the Southeast.

BIM allows the design team and clients to see inside a building. This diagnostic ability greatly reduces errors, and identifies potential conflicts before construction begins. Even after construction is complete, the model lives on through its functionality for building operations and facilities management.

The value of BIM has been clearly demonstrated on four recently completed projects: The International Longshoremen's Office building, Port Royal Retail Center, Armstrong Atlantic State University's Continuing Education Center and Sea Island Bank Drayton Street Branch. BIM increased coordination during design and construction, reduced requests for information and change orders, and enhanced client communications and provided valuable marketing imagery.

Sustainability is a common thread in all projects. The green-building approach offers a tremendous opportunity to reduce the environmental impact of construction while producing healthier indoor environment and lowering operating costs. Lott + Barber Architects use an integrated design approach to create green buildings that are resource-efficient, environmentally sound and fiscally responsible. The sustainable design approach extends into the community by considering issues such as stormwater management, historic preservation, mixed use design, and other components. In addition to principals Forrest R. Lott, AIA and Scott A. Barber, AIA, architect Steve Stowers, AIA, and planner Denise Grabowski, AICP are LEED™ Accredited Professionals by the U.S. Green Building Council.

Savannah Technical College Liberty County Campus, Hinesville, Georgia

Hussey, Gay, Bell & DeYoung, Inc.

Founded in Savannah, Georgia in 1958, and has grown to be one of the top *Engineering News-Record 500* leaders.

River Street

Hussey, Gay, Bell & DeYoung (HGBD) provides a full range of services from our staff of over 150 professionals and technicians. HGBD has provided design and construction overview in the field of infrastructure, defense, water and wastewater, industrial, civil, structural, marine, environmental services, architecture, interior design, and landscape architecture as well as support services in the fields of geotechnical, and surveying. Founded in Savannah, Georgia in 1958, we have steadily grown to be one of the top *Engineering News-Record 500* leaders. Currently the firm has offices located in Savannah and Atlanta, Georgia as well as Columbia and Charleston, South Carolina. During HGBD's forty-seven year history we have completed projects in 25 U.S. States and 17 Countries.

HGBD has built a large clientele of municipalities throughout the years representing over 35 municipalities, public service districts and authorities. The firm has complete many historic revitalization projects including Savannah's Rousakis Plaza (River Street) project which transformed a decaying riverfront area into an attractive waterfront pedestrian concourse. Additional consideration was given to preservation of the esthetic value of the buildings landward of the riverfront

which ranged in age from 70 to 150 years. Because of this project, shops, restaurants, and inns have opened in great numbers in the cotton warehouses which stood empty on the River Street level for many years. Bicycle paths, concert areas, display areas and small boat mooring facilities were incorporated into the design. The Plaza and its concourse has become a major attraction for both visitors and local residents, and a focal point for outdoor concerts, art shows, and festivals. In addition, the second phase of the project was used for the opening ceremonies for the 1996 Olympic Sailing venue.

With Savannah's steady growth over the past fifty years, many large companies are taking advantage of the opportunities offered by having a thriving port, rail system,

and close proximity to Interstates 95 and 16. One of the more recent companies that have moved to this fast growing area is J.C. Bamford Excavators LTD. Located in Pooler, Georgia the design/build, 500,000- square-foot manufacturing facility was a turnkey project that utilized HGBD's civil, industrial, environmental, geotechnical and structural engineering as will as architectural design and construction management services. In addition to the manufacturing section of the plant, the facility includes 90,000 square feet of office space, a training facility, a cafeteria, and a theater. The building's 1,100-acre site provides area for future expansions and satellite industries. An 18-acre lake with fountains and display islands is accessed by underwater bridges and parking facilities. HGBD's industrial engineers evaluated J.C. Bamford's existing manu facturing facilities in the United Kingdom and worked with the

client to refine a fitting process for its U.S. tractor assembly plant.

During the growth of Savannah's tourism and business community, HGBD has had a major role in the upgrading of the infrastructure feeding this economy. Since 1962, HGBD has been responsible for the upgrades and modifications of Savannah's Industrial & Domestic Water System (I&D). The I&D water filtration plant draws surface water from Abercorn Creek, a tributary of the Savannah River, approximately seven miles west of the plant. The treatment plant's large 48-inch diameter transmission mains serve the industries along the Savannah River and boost water pressure in the City of Savannah's distribution system by connections at various points in the city. HGBD's experience with the City of Savannah ranges from upgrades at the 50 MGD water treatment plant design of many of the City's wastewater treatment plants, water & sewer line work, various transportation projects, and the City's Dean Forrest Road Landfill.

On each project, regardless of the services being employed, HGBD demonstrates its dedication to the client. HGBD's staff members work with the client throughout the project to meet design, budget and time requirements. A full support staff is assigned to each job to guarantee smooth design and production. All design professionals assigned to each project continue in their roles through project completion to ensure continuity of design and respond to any questions or concerns that may arise.

While offering a variety of services to clients, HGBD does not sacrifice quality. The firm has won National and State awards for various projects in the past, including the 1999 Excellence in Architecture Award by the National School Board Association for its work on Savannah High School. In 1997, HGBD won the Excellence in Engineering Award from the Consulting Engineers of South Carolina for the East Cooper River Water Project Direction Drill.

Its diversity has served Hussey, Gay, Bell & DeYoung well, and its success continues to this day. The company stays strong due to the large amount of growth in the coastal Georgia and South Carolina areas. As that growth continues, so will HGBD's success in providing excellent engineering and architectural services for the job.

Armstrong Atlantic State University

When the city fathers of Savannah founded Armstrong Junior College in 1935, they couldn't know that seventy years later it would become the largest public institution of higher education in the community.

The municipally supported college was initially housed in a magnificent gray brick Italianate Renaissance mansion, the Armstrong House, a generous gift to the city from the family of George F. Armstrong, a successful Savannah shipping businessman. Over the years, the college would spread into six additional buildings in the area adjacent to the Forsyth Park and Monterey Square areas. The imposing Armstrong mansion and the surrounding neighborhood provided the new junior college with its distinctive character for the next thirty years.

The college opened its doors with 168 first-year students and eight faculty and staff members. In June 1937, seventy-eight students became the first graduates of the new college. The first president of the college, Ernest A. Lowe, came to Savannah from the University of Georgia and from the offices of the newly formed University System of Georgia (USG).

President Foreman Hawes led the college through the war years and the years that followed when the returning veterans greatly expanded the institution's enrollment. In 1959, as Armstrong College of Savannah, the institution became a two-year unit of the USG. In 1964, the Board of Regents conferred four-year status on Armstrong State College.

As the college was outgrowing the confines of the Historic District, it moved to the south side in 1966 thanks to a magnanimous gift of land from Donald Livingston and the Mills B. Lane Foundation. There, "where Abercorn Street ended," the college began to expand further, adding new buildings, new degrees, professional and graduate programs. In 1996, the institution gained state university status and yet another new name: Armstrong Atlantic State University (AASU).

Top photo: Armstrong Atlantic State University President Thomas Z. Jones

Lower photo: The Science Center is the newest academic building.

Through all the changes, Armstrong Atlantic has stayed true to its rich tradition, focusing on a firm commitment to the ideals of a liberal education. As a result, the university has graduated many who are now the region's leading attorneys, businessmen, physicians, scientists, healthcare professionals, a mayor, eighty percent of local nurses and non-physician medical staff, and over half of the area's Teachers of the Year.

Students are introduced to state-of-the-art laboratories.

Throughout his seventeen years of leadership (1982-1999), President Robert A. Burnett successfully guided the college through periods of both great challenge and attainment. The school's endowment skyrocketed, two new buildings rose, twenty-five academic majors were born, and ground was broken for the Science Center and the first on-campus student residence community.

With the arrival of President Thomas Z. Jones in 2000, new initiatives began to take shape. Building upon the strong academic foundations laid by his predecessors, Jones projected a vision that included a culture of leadership education beginning with students, extending through the faculty and staff, and reaching into the community. He ushered in an era of public-private partnerships that resulted in the creation of the Armstrong Center, additional on-campus student housing, and a student recreation center.

Armstrong Atlantic State University offers more than seventy-five challenging degrees, minors, and certificates in the College of Arts and Sciences, the College of Education, the College of Health Professions, the School of Computing, and the School of Graduate Studies.

Pre-professional programs in ,business, dentistry, engineering, forestry, law, medicine, pharmacy, physical therapy and veterinary medicine are also offered. Additionally, students may begin at Armstrong Atlantic to earn a Georgia Tech baccalaureate degree in computer (software), civil, mechanical, or electrical engineering without ever leaving Savannah. The Commission on Colleges of the Southern Association of Colleges and Schools accredits the university to award associate's, baccalaureate, and master's degrees.

Academic facilities include state of the art computer and science labs, multimedia classrooms, writing and advisement centers, math tutorial labs, a greenhouse, and an Honors Program suite.

AASU also offers degree programs in Glynn and Liberty counties and provides courses on an as-needed basis throughout its service area.

The university serves the local community with an extensive array of professional and continuing education programs from professional development and self-improvement classes to worldwide travel opportunities. A conference facility at the Armstrong Center features meeting rooms, auditorium, banquet facilities, and a ballroom that serves medium size events for a wide variety of interest groups.

Another service to the community has been the relocation of the Dental Hygiene Clinic, and the RiteCare Center for Communication Disorders to the nearby Savannah Mall.

Since its inception, the university has been a valuable cultural resource to the region. Today, three theaters and an art gallery house an expansive array of cultural events showcasing lectures, festivals, musical performances, and art exhibits. The Masquers, a theatrical company dating back to the early years of the college, presents a full range of classics, contemporary plays, and musicals.

An impressive NCAA Division II intercollegiate athletic program encompasses basketball, softball, baseball, volleyball, soccer, tennis, and golf.

Sports facilities include a student recreation center, lighted tennis courts, a baseball diamond, an indoor heated swimming pool, a sand volleyball court, several playing fields, an indoor running track, two basketball courts, and fully-equipped exercise and weightrooms. Students may participate in more than sixty student clubs, leadership programs, professional groups, academic honor societies, and Greek organizations. The diverse population includes students representing nearly all fifty states, the District of Columbia, and more than 70 countries.

The university's 268-acre campus is beautifully landscaped and designated as an arboretum. The arboretum displays more than 1,100 species of trees, shrubs, and other woody plants. The campus contains both native and introduced species of trees and shrubs, the majority of which are labeled. Gardening groups, school children, and the general public frequently tour the arboretum's varied collections including the International Garden which features plants from all over the world and an outdoor amphitheater.

Armstrong Atlantic State University has come a long way since its founding in 1935. One can only imagine what the future will bring to this vibrant, burgeoning campus and to the region it serves.

Many Armstrong Atlantic alumni are now leaders in the region.

ST. JOSEPH'S/CANDLER
Historic Significance. Modern Marvel.

St. Joseph's/Candler has an unrivaled heritage of caring for the citizens of Savannah. St. Joseph's Hospital and Candler Hospital are the oldest healthcare institutions in southeast Georgia. These two formidable health institutions joined forces in 1997. Combined, the hospitals have nearly 400 years of service to the people of Georgia's Coastal Empire and South Carolina's Low Country. Now known as St. Joseph's/Candler (SJ/C) it is the only faith-based, not-for-profit health care provider in the region providing breakthrough technology to rival virtually any health care facility in the county.

St. Joseph's Hospital

The origins of St. Joseph's Hospital can be traced to 1845 when the Dublin, Ireland-based Catholic Sisters of Mercy arrived in Savannah and founded St. Vincent's Academy for girls. The Sisters' commitment to the poor and underserved took on another dimension three decades later when they were contracted by the U.S. government to care for sick seamen, and took over the operations of the Forest City Marine Hospital.

One year later, the hospital moved to a new building in downtown Savannah and the name was changed to St. Joseph's Infirmary. In 1901, it became St. Joseph's Hospital.

Through the years, St. Joseph's Hospital would grow and adapt to meet the needs of the residents of Savannah. St. John's Hall, the city's first psychiatric unit, opened during the early 1950s, a decade that also saw the hospital establish Savannah's first obstetrical clinic for the poor.

Witnessing Savannah's population explosion during the 1960's, the Sisters of Mercy looked to the city's spacious south side for a site to build a new seven-story St. Joseph's Hospital, settling on 28 acres where the 305-bed, acute care facility resides today.

The move did not foster a sense of complacency, however.

By 1977, St. Joseph's Hospital had a specialty in Oto-Neurology treating patients with visual, spinal cord, brain and brainstem injuries and disorders. In 1981, the facility opened Savannah's first ambulatory care center. And in 1986, open-heart surgery was added it its repertoire of services. The hospital has become the recognized leader in cardiovascular care as well as neurosciences, orthopedics.

The original location of Savannah's healthcare leaders: St. Josephs' Hospital (top) on the corner of Habersham and Taylor Streets and Candler Hospital (bottom) near the corner of Gaston and Drayton Streets.

Candler Hospital

Candler Hospital, meanwhile, is the second-oldest continuously operating hospital in the United States.

The facility's history dates to the 1730s when a Methodist missionary George Whitfield, brought large quantities of medicine to the British colonie's vital port city of Savannah "for the cure of sickness."

Whitfield's widely admired work with the sick and infirmed during the 18th Century led eventually and directly to the creation of Georgia's first formal healthcare facility, the Savannah Poor House and Hospital, chartered on December 12, 1804. The hospital would operate out of a private home in downtown Savannah until 1819.

Many years later, in 1872, the facility dropped the poorhouse designation from its name and became known as Savannah Hospital, which hosted the Savannah School of Medicine, and also the city's first school of nursing.

The Nancy N. and J. C. Lewis Cancer and Research Pavilion (above).

State-of the art technology at The Heart Hospital.

The Savannah Hospital would keep its moniker until 1930, when it was acquired by the Georgia Hospital Board of Methodist Episcopal Church South, which promptly changed the name of the hospital to honor the then local bishop, Warren A. Candler.

Later, in 1960, Candler Hospital would take under its wing The Telfair Hospital for Females, founded in 1886, and the nation's oldest women's hospital; it would eventually become Candler's obstetrical unit and grow to include a myriad of women's specialty services.

Then, in 1980, Candler Hospital moved to its current location on Reynolds Street in midtown Savannah, where it now serves the healthcare needs of its ninth and tenth generation of families in Georgia's First City.

ST. JOSEPH'S/CANDLER

In 1997, St. Joseph's Hospital and Candler Hospital entered into a joint operating agreement that united the city's two premier healthcare organizations.

Together, its two anchor institutions, St. Joseph's Hospital and Candler Hospital, provide the highest quality primary and specialized care, treating illness and promoting wellness throughout the region. Both hospital institutions have been individually accredited by the Joint Commission on Accreditation of Health Care Organizations (JCAHO), while jointly, the health system is one of only a few in the country to have received JCAHO network accreditation status. St. Joseph's/Candler is also the recipient of the Magnet Award for nursing excellence, one of only a select few healthcare organizations in the country to have achieved such preeminent status.

SMART CARE + SMART TECH-NOLGY = SMART MEDICINE

Today, the compassionate care that created these two legendary health icons continues, along side its prestige of offering unsurpassed space-age technology and expert clinical care.

St. Joseph's campus is home to such specialized services as The Heart Hospital, The Institute for Advanced Bone and Joint Surgery and the Institute of Neurosciences, each offering the latest and most advanced medical procedures and treatments.

Candler has been long recognized as offering the finest in primary care, outpatient services and women's and children's services. Candler Hospital is home to the Mary Telfair Women's Hospital, the region's undisputed leader in advanced obstetrical, gynecological, education and outpatient services for women. The Nancy N. and J.C Lewis Cancer and Research Pavilion, which opened in late 2005, is affiliated with the NCI designated Moffitt Cancer Center and Research Institute in Tampa, Florida and provides patients with access to some of the most advanced oncology services in the country.

In addition to the above stated signature services, the health system also offers advanced care in areas of imaging, gastroenterology, pulmonary, sports medicine, geriatrics, wellness services, diabetes treatment and management, outpatient surgical services, and emergency care.

An underlying philosophy at St. Joseph's/Candler is to remain ahead of the technology curve. Access to the latest advancements in research, treatment and technology are paramount ingredients to successful patient outcomes and overall patient experience. St. Joseph's/Candler's modern, futuristic approach to technology assists our physicians, surgeons and clinical staff in providing the patient with only the highest quality of care.

For more information on any of the services offered at St. Joseph's/Candler, please contact CareCall at
(912) 819-3360 or 1-800-622-6877

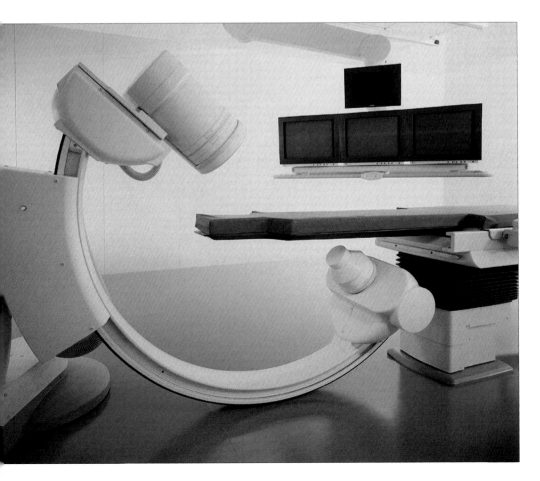

Thomas & Hutton Engineering Co.

Co/Founder Mr. Hue Thomas

Co/Founder Mr. Joseph J. Hutton

Thomas & Hutton Engineering Co. was founded in 1946 by Hue Thomas and Joseph J. Hutton in the beautiful city of Savannah, Georgia. Mr. Thomas and Mr. Hutton anticipated tremendous opportunities in providing professional consulting engineering services to private entities and city and county municipalities seeking to develop the local area. Today, the firm is one of the oldest and most respected engineering firms in Savannah as it continues to lead the way in the redevelopment of the local historic downtown areas, the growth in residential communities and commercial/retail/industrial sites, and infrastructure improvements that make Savannah an exciting area to live and work. The firm has branched out and is a key contributor in the bustling revitalization and the continued development throughout coastal Georgia and the Carolina region.

Mr. Thomas and Mr. Hutton believed that in order to achieve success, a work culture had to be created pertaining to the issues of personnel, operations, cost control, and responsiveness to client concerns. These core values are best summarized in the firm's mission statement: **Relationships and Solutions for Success.**

At its commencement, the partnership was named Thomas & Hutton, Engineers and provided engineering services exclusively related to surveying,

Mr. William Foster

wastewater, and water systems. In 1955, a new entity, Thomas & Hutton Engineering, Co., was incorporated to provide civil engineering services, while the partnership, Thomas & Hutton, Engineers remained solely for management purposes. The partnership (Thomas & Hutton, Engineers) was dissolved in the late 1970's and Thomas & Hutton Engineering Co. has expanded its services and transitioned into the full-service consulting engineering firm we now know today.

Mr. Thomas and Mr. Hutton instilled exceptional work ethics and core values that still remain fundamental to the

firm and its employees. With the retirement of Mr. Thomas and Mr. Hutton, their successors, Vreeland George and William Foster, Sr. carried on the legacy of making Thomas & Hutton one of the best engineering firms in the southeast. With its corporate headquarters located in Savannah, Thomas & Hutton has branch offices in Charleston and Myrtle Beach, South Carolina, Wilmington, North Carolina, and St. Simons Island, Georgia. Once they retired in the late 1990's, leadership was passed on to the next generation and present-day management. Danny Stanley is the current President and Chief Executive Officer, Mitchell Bohannon is Chairman of the Board and Chief Operating Officer, and Samuel McCachern is Sr. Vice President and Chief Financial Officer. These three professional engineers make up Thomas & Hutton's Executive Committee.

Thomas & Hutton has grown from a small firm of two to its present-day staff of over 375 and the firm is steadily growing as the Savannah area continue to thrive.

The firm's project work revolves around the following disciplines: large-scale planned communities, residential and resort community development, land planning, landscape architecture, commercial/retail/industrial sites, institutional facilities, transportation and roads, storm

Mr. Vreeland George

water management, water and wastewater systems, structural engineering, marine facilities, surveying, and GIS. The firm's employees are actively involved in all planning and design tasks. All projects are efficiently developed from planning and permitting phases through construction management and operations certification. Thomas & Hutton has worked on numerous projects over the years that have helped Savannah and its surrounding areas become a unique place to work and live. In the firms initial years, Savannah's roads were unimproved and wastewater systems discharged its effluent directly into the

Savannah River. Thomas & Hutton's earliest extensive projects consisted of road, water, and wastewater system designs for the city of Savannah to improve its existing conditions. Thomas & Hutton also worked on the original warehouse and has done numerous expansion projects and distribution facilities for one of its oldest clients, Chatham Steel. Thomas & Hutton was also involved with the original design for Memorial Hospital and continues to be a partner in the additions to the medical campus by working on the Cardiac Institute and the Research and Education Building for what is now known as Memorial Medical Health University Medical Center.

In the span of 60 years, the firm has also been involved in ventures that include military projects comprising of airfields, weapon ranges, and even fall-out shelters during the midst of the Cold War, impressive site development projects such as Sea Pines (Hilton Head Island, South Carolina), Sea Island (St. Simons Island, Georgia), The Landings on Skidaway Island (Savannah, Georgia), Palmetto Bluff (Bluffton, South Carolina), Kiawah Island, South Carolina, and Daniel Island (Charleston, South Carolina), and Prince Creek (Myrtle Beach).

Thomas & Hutton's projects making dynamic impacts in the region include the Georgia International Trade and Convention

Center and new residential and commercial mixed-use developments, such as the Savannah Riverfront developments, the Tanger Oulet in Charleston, South Carolina, and the Market Commons in Myrtle Beach, South Carolina.

Other projects that reflect Thomas & Hutton's capabilities include the Chatham County Economic Development Site, Wal-Mart Supercenters, Crossroads Business Park, which will bring jobs and opportunities to the region. In addition, Thomas & Hutton performed engineering services for several institutional facilities such as Georgia Tech's Technology and Engineering Campus, Armstrong Atlantic State University, Savannah State University, and local public and private schools.

Also critical to the area's growth are the major transportation and roadway projects that Thomas & Hutton has been involved with including Diamond Causeway, Jimmy DeLoach Parkway, and Pooler Parkway/I-16 Interchange.

Thomas & Hutton is dedicated to providing the professional service and solutions that its clients have come to expect and receives over 85% of its work through repeat business.

In addition to the strong external client relationships, the positive internal relationships made among Thomas & Hutton employees is a contributing factor to the firm's rank of 7th Best Mid-Size Civil Engineering Firm to Work for and the 14th Best Engineering Firm to Work for in the nation by CE News in 2005.

Thomas & Hutton is committed to giving back to the community. Its employees are actively involved in various civic organizations and causes such as the American Red Cross, American Heart Association, Leadership Savannah, United Way, Royce Learning Center/Adult Literacy, YMCA, Rotary International, Habitat for Humanity, Make-A-Wish Foundation, Rape Crisis Center, and other various charity organizations. In addition to the firm's involvement with charitable organizations, Thomas & Hutton proudly supports numerous cultural and sporting events in the area.

A thriving operation since 1946, Thomas & Hutton Engineering Co. is extremely optimistic about the region's and the firm's future. With decades of experience and the anticipation of many more to come, Thomas & Hutton's future holds great expectations as it continues to rise on its upward path of growth and success.

Left to right: Sam McCachern, (Sr. Vice President & CFO), Mitchell Bohannon (Chairman of the Board & COO), & Danny Stanley (President & CEO).

Georgia Gastroenterology Group, PC
Georgia Center for Digestive Diseases, LLC

With the distinction of being the largest solo gastroenterology practice in the southern United States, the Georgia Gastroenterology Group, PC is dedicated to the diagnosis and treatment of adults with digestive illnesses.

Leading the group is medical director, Dr. Nicholas V. Costrini, a board-certified internist and gastroenterologist, who completed a medical internship, residency and both gastrointestinal and molecular biology fellowships at the Washington University School of Medicine in Missouri. He also holds a doctorate in physiology from Marquette University in Wisconsin.

Dr. Costrini is highly regarded for numerous contributions to the field of medicine on both regional and national levels and adds accomplished author and editor to his resume as he has been published in a wide variety of medical literature collections.

But it is in reality his skill, combined with a unique philosophical and artistic approach to medicine that has won his practice legions.

A regular health columnist of "Good For What Ails You," which is published by the Savannah Morning News, Dr. Costrini's appreciation of literature, music, theatre and movement often make an appearance in his medical and business operations.

Dr. Costrini and his staff, which include physician extenders and nurses as well as a professional administrative body, who individually bring many years of experience to their various roles, host an annual series entitled "Music and Medicine," free to the public. The series serves as a platform to discuss relevant and important medical topics, while showcasing various musical artists as the items of conversation. Concerts by those same artists follow the discussions, which have incorporated themes ranging from the

compositions of Ludwig van Beethoven, the literature of Ernest Hemingway and the choreography genius of George Balanchine.

The doctor also supports research development in the area of Inflammatory Bowel Disease by funding an annual competitive research grant program at his alma mater, Washington University.

The Georgia Gastroenterology Group on the whole is known for its outward reaching medical staff, whose core of professionalism is deeply rooted to revolve around the respect of its patients. From the appearance of the waiting rooms, which are detailed with fine furnishings and artwork, to the time spent with each individual so that they understand the ins and outs of complex medicine, this practice goes beyond the normal level of service to gain patients' trust and assure their comfort.

Another important element in the philosophy of the group is Dr. Costrini's availability. The solo physician model allows patients to reach the doctor at almost all hours of the day if needed. Whether it's 10:00 a.m. or 10:00 p.m. patients are very likely to reach Dr. Costrini himself for a phone consultation at minimum. This unique aspect of Georgia Gastroenterology Group has served as the basis of its growth in recent years.

There are now extended services with the addition of The Georgia Center for Digestive Diseases, which came about in 2000. The state-of-the-art ambulatory surgery center located in the same building as Georgia Gastroenterolgoy Group specializes in gastrointestinal endoscopic procedures and is equipped with advanced technology that allows Dr. Costrini to detect and diagnose digestive problems. Services offered in the Center include upper endoscopy, flexible sigmoidoscopy, colonoscopy (screening and diagnostic) and endoscopic unltrasound.

The Center also offers visitors a private and skilled outpatient center operative that focuses on safety, comfort and personal attention that many larger institutions often lack. Nationally accredited and state-licensed, the highly-trained staff members exclusively care for patients with adult digestive diseases. From the patients arrival to their departure the priority is to make their experience as relaxed and comfortable as possible while receiving the best level of healthcare service possible.

In 2005, Dr. Costrini further dedicated a part of the office to an Inflammatory Bowel Disease Center where patients with IBD are able to receive treatment and infusions in comfort and privacy with the personal attention of a skilled IBD nurse.

As a result of Dr. Costrini's effective and all-encompassing direction, he was inducted into the Fellowship of the American Gastroenterological Association (AGAF) in May of 2006. An honor bestowed upon those with superior professional achievements in practice and/or research in the field of gastroenterology, Dr. Costrini has rightfully earned such a distinction.

The Georgia Gastroenterology Group and The Georgia Center for Digestive Diseases continue to strive to provide state-of-the-art diagnostic and therapeutic care for all aspects of gastrointestinal medicine and nutrition.

Sitting on 173 acres in Savannah and Thunderbolt, Savannah State University nestles on the bluff of an arm of the sea extending inland to meet the mouth of the Wilmington River. Students in the university's acclaimed marine sciences program utilize the bordering salt marsh as their second classroom, and a dock located behind the marine sciences wet laboratory leads to multiple vessels that are used by students to explore the coastal waterways of Savannah. The university's unique and picturesque location is one that sets the institution apart.

Savannah State University

While it continues to advance with the ever-changing times to provide its 3,100 students with academic excellence, Sanannah State University is proud of its rich history. The oldest public historically black college in the state, the institution was founded in 1890 in Athens as Georgia State Industrial College for Colored Youth. The college moved to its beloved coastal Georgia location in 1891. The university's first president was Major Richard R. Wright, Sr., who served from 1891-1921. The school became a full-time degree granting institution in 1928, and four years later, Georgia State Industrial College for Colored Youth was renamed Georgia State College and was named Savannah State College in 1950. Being in the historic, gracious city of Savannah has allowed the institution to flourish; Savannah State University has grown a community of alumni, supporters, faculty and staff that resembles a close-knit family.

Savannah State University, with one of the most diverse faculty within the University System of Georgia, has three colleges: the College of Business Administration, the College of Liberal Arts and Social Sciences and the College of Sciences and Technology. Within those colleges, four of 23 undergraduate degree programs have been designated Centers of Academic Excellence based on quality, student demand and market relevance. These include marine sciences, mass communications, computer information systems and social work.

As part of the university's commitment to make an impact on the Savannah area, students are encouraged to venture off campus for internships and community service opportunities. Combining classroom lessons and real-life settings, students in the university's

College of Business Administration, which is accredited by the Association to Advance Collegiate Schools of Business International, complete internship assignments at various organizations in Savannah, including the Savannah Entrepreneurial Center. Launched by the city of Savannah with Savannah State University's assistance, the center provides customized training for individuals who want to start, expand or maintain a small business operation. The Savannah Entrepreneurial Center is located in downtown Savannah.

A number of Savannah State University's students have had opportunities to visit foreign lands such as Ghana, Brazil, China, India and the Caribbean. Through the International Education Center, students are able to study abroad where they learn about the topics they study in classes, but learn even more outside classrooms through exposure to the global society. Students gain a better understanding of various cultures and human diversity.

The university offers the Naval Reserve Officers Training Corps (NROTC) program designed to prepare the student for a commission in the U.S. Navy or Marine Corps. Students at Savannah State University can also participate in the Georgia Tech Regional Engineering Program, where students take classes at SSU and graduate with a degree from Georgia Tech in civil, computer, electrical or mechanical engineering.

The Survey Research Center, a division of the Office of Graduate Studies and Sponsored Research, is located on the campus of Savannah State University. The Survey Research Center began operations in 1996 and was established to meet the growing data collection and analysis needs of businesses and government

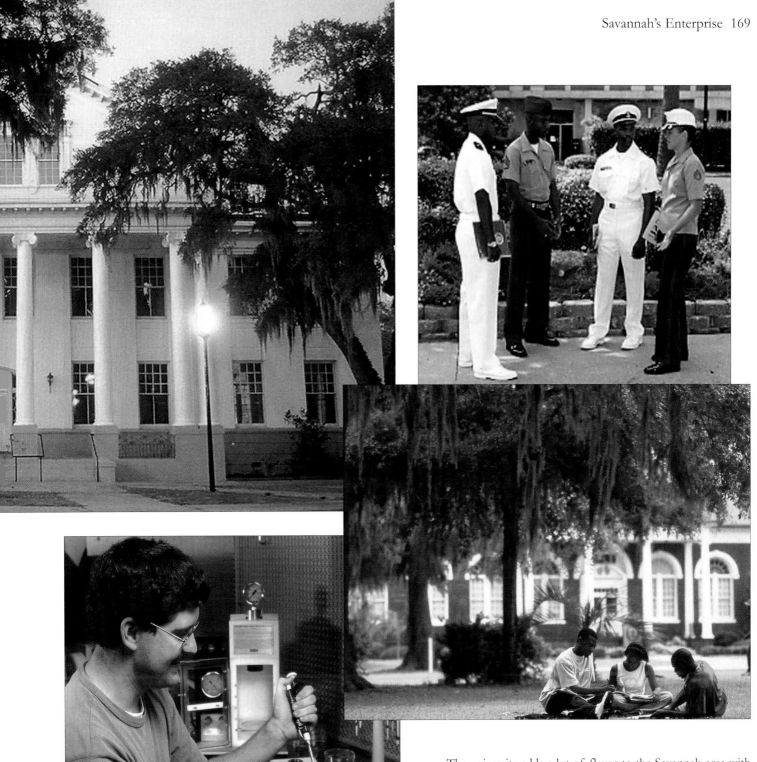

organizations in the Southeast. It has expanded to meet the demands of out-of-state customers and serves as a research resource for the university's faculty.

Savannah State University impacts the local economy by approximately $90 million (fiscal year 2004). Commissioned by the University System of Georgia's (USG) Intellectual Capital Partnership Program (ICAPP), the 2004 study was conducted by the Selig Center for Economic Growth in the University of Georgia's Terry College of Business. The institution's economic impact is actually greater than the study reveals due to spending by retirees in the region covered who were not included in the study. Universities have long-term impacts on the labor force, local business and industry and local government.

The university adds a lot of flavor to the Savannah area with its NCAA [National Collegiate Athletic Association] Division I sport teams. Each year, the university's Homecoming celebration and football game, held in the fall, draws a crowd of 15,000 alumni, visitors and Savannah residents to the campus.

The annual Savannah Black Heritage Festival, another happening that draws large crowds, is presented by the city of Savannah's Department of Cultural Affairs and Savannah State University. This series of events highlighting the cultural and artistic contributions of African-Americans takes place on the Savannah State University campus and various venues around Savannah, such as the Lucas Theatre and the Savannah Civic Center. Sponsored by the city of Savannah since 1989, the festival has been produced by the university since 1999.

Savannah State University is matchless in its academic excellence, its charm and beauty, its family-oriented force, its warm spirit and its small-town feel with urban access. With these combined characteristics, students understand *they can get anywhere from here*.

Savannah's Elegant Sisters: The Mulberry Inn

The award-winning Mulberry Inn is considered to be one of Savannah's finest and most elegant hotels. Throughout the building there are period furnishings, oil paintings, polished hardwood floors, and delicate chandeliers that offer a glimpse into the hotel's past.

The inn, which sits on Savannah's historic Washington Square, was originally built of handmade bricks in 1860 and served as a cotton warehouse and livery stable. In the early 1900's, the site transformed into the second Coca-Cola Bottling Company in the United States.

It wasn't until 1982 that the structure again changed hands and was converted into an unassuming hotel. However, during the 1990's the inn witnessed its own radical upgrade, as it was purchased and placed under the auspices of Holiday Inn Hotels, a subsidiary of the Intercontinental Hotel Group. Much to the group's credit, the historical significance of the hotel was appreciated and destined to retain the inn's distinct charm.

Consequently, the building's original design was recovered and enhanced with restoration work, including that of the hotel's brick-covered patio, which is now replete with fountains, trailing ivy, and wrought-iron furniture. However, it is the lobby that is the grand dame with gleaming heart-pine floors and period antiques, including a handsome English grandfather clock and an exquisitely carved Victorian mantel.

Each day between 4:00 and 6:00 p.m. the lobby hosts the ever-popular Afternoon Tea, at which guests nibble on desserts and sip from a wide variety of teas and coffees while listening to a live pianist

Other amenities include an outdoor pool, hot tub, fitness center, and concierge while guestrooms and suites, 145 in total, are quaint and inviting. Blending the best of historical Savannah and modern necessities, the inn also specializes in weddings, banquets, meetings and other special events with facilities that accommodate up to 150 people.

The Hampton Inn

As an unofficial sister hotel to the Mulberry Inn, The Hampton Inn,
is also situated in Savannah's historic district and adjacent to the world famous River Street.
It is also within walking distance to the center's hub, City Market,
as well as a wide range of boutique shops and eclectic restaurants.

As a further testament to the value that the Hampton Inn places on preservation and promotion, the local inn blends in seamlessly with its surrounding historical architecture. Authentic Savannah gray brick walls and a hotel lobby furnished with antiques and restored heart pine floors lend to a distinctly southern experience.

However, modern amenities are not forgotten. The inn also offers a complimentary hot breakfast buffet, high-speed internet access and USA Today each Monday through Friday. There are also meeting rooms, a fitness center, an outdoor roof-top pool with a spectacular view of the Savannah River, a concierge service, laundry/valet service and porter service. The enhanced guests rooms feature special king rooms and double rooms with microwaves and refrigerators while the warm surroundings and friendly service are backed by a 100 percent Hampton Satisfaction Guarantee – if a customers are not completely satisfied with their stay, they don't pay.

Not surprisingly, the local outfit of the Hampton Inn, in conjunction with The Mulberry Inn, also supports grass roots efforts in Savannah's historical preservation movement. Together they have sponsored events with such organizations as the Georgia Historical Society.

While the Hampton Inn is a modern structure that opened in January 1997, it derives from a long lineage of conservation-minded enthusiasts. With the help of hundreds of dedicated hotel volunteers, the inn's parent company, Hilton Hotels, was recently awarded with the *Preserve America* Presidential Award for its world-renowned Save-a-Landmark initiative. The company's efforts have cost nearly $2 million dollars throughout its campaign to save 26 U.S. landmarks over a span of six years. As the first hotel chain ever recognized by a U.S. President, Hampton Hotel executives recently received the prestigious award from President George W. Bush at a ceremony at the White House.

Erickson Associates, Inc.

Theodore "Ted" Erickson was a quiet,
yet an influential man, who set the
standard for customer and employee
loyalty when he began Erickson's,
Inc., a small contracting firm that
has provided mechanical
contracting to clients throughout
the southeast since 1950. After
Ted Erickson completed his tour
of duty with the Navy, he
returned to Savannah committed to
the advancement of the city he
loved and acted as a major force in
attracting business
and educational opportunities.

Erickson was part of the group from Savannah that helped bring Grumman (now Gulfstream Aero Space) to the area, worked diligently with the airport commission and the Savannah Economic development Authority, and acted as one of the original founders of The Savannah Country Day School. While Ted Erickson preferred to work behind the scenes, his contribution to the Savannah area was great. He took much pleasure and pride in the accomplishments of his business, community and family. Erickson's determination, creativity, and involvement succeeded in building solid relationships that launched the Erickson legacy that stands strong today.

"You can't outrun your sergeants," Erickson used to say. And until his death in 2002, he always strived to surround himself with loyal, trustworthy individuals who could lead well and maintain the level of integrity and trust expected. Erickson's successor, William C. (Clate) Ralston, Jr. has been employed by the Erickson Group since graduating from Georgia Tech in 1964. Ralston has extensive experience in project management, design-build projects, as well as, competitive bid projects that include hospitals, office buildings, civic centers, jails, housing projects, nuclear power plants and other specialty projects.

During his four-decade span, Ralston has worked in various positions, ranging from company expeditor to Vice President to his current role as President and CEO of Erickson Associates, Inc. The transition occurred in September of 2004 when Ralston became the principal shareholder of the group. The remaining ownership is shared with Theodore W. Erickson, Jr., who acts as President of the mechanical division of the company, with primary responsibilities in sales and mechanical construction management, and Brad Harris, who is currently Vice President, responsible for the management of Specialty Construction and the Service Department. Both Erickson, Jr. and Harris have been with the Erickson Group since 1979.

Theordore W. Erickson, Jr.
President Mechanical
Division,
1979-Present (27 years
with the Company)

Photo top left:
Theodore W. Erickson,
Founder & CEO
1949-2002 (53 years with
the Company)

Photo top right:
Edward Bradley Harris
Vice President
Specialty Construction
& Service
1979-Present (27 years
with the Company)

William C. Ralston, Jr.
President/CEO/COB
1964-Present (42 years with the Company)

Erickson Associates, Inc. has performed mechanical construction for a wide variety of projects, large and small, technical and non-technical. Yet throughout all of them, this owner-operated company has strived to maintain steady and controlled growth with great emphasis on commitment to quality and sound ethical business principles that trickle from the top down. This commitment is maintained through closely held ownership promoting management that is consistent with these principles. Senior management remains active in daily business affairs of the company and offers strong training programs for all employees to further promote corporate ideals.

Licensed in Georgia and South Carolina, Erickson Associates, Inc.'s construction expertise is primarily in the health care, institutional, commercial, and industrial markets. A significant portion of the company's workload typically involves the installation of mechanical systems and central energy plants. Erickson Associates, Inc. also pledges that each project will be assigned key managers who are entrusted with the responsibility and authority to make informed decisions and work closely with clients and their respective architects and engineers to achieve the fundamental goals of quality, safety and cost-efficiency. Follow-up services for clients are also vitally important for mechanical systems. Therefore, the company maintains a Service Department, offering a full range of routine service maintenance plans, as well as tailor-made plans to meet any customer's need. As a result, Erickson Associates, Inc. has proudly accepted numerous safety awards and praises from satisfied customers who compliment the company's ability to manage complex projects, specifically citing the highly sensitive healthcare environment, without interruption of ongoing patient care.

In fact, one need not look further than the roster of clientele for whom Erickson Associates, Inc. has performed multiple mechanical projects. They stand as evidence of the quality of workmanship and the integrity of the company. Clients include Savannah WestinResort Hotel, the Georgia Maritime and International Trade Center in Savannah, the South Georgia Medical Center in Valdosta, the Hilton Head Medical Center and Clinics, Hunter/Ft. Stewart, Memorial Health University Medical Center, St. Joseph's/Candler Healthcare Systems, Palmer & Cay, Gulfstream Aerospace Corporation, and the DeSoto Hilton Hotel, among many others.

However, in an ever evolving industry, Erickson Associates, Inc. continually looks forward to keeping abreast of industry changes and holds association memberships with Mechanical Contractors Association of American (MCAA), American Society of Heating, Refrigerating and Air Conditioning Engineers, Inc. (ASRAE), National Certified Pipe Welding Bureau (NCPWB), National Association of Plumbing, Heating and Cooling Contractors (NAPHCC) and the Georgia Society of Healthcare Engineers to do so.

Eyes on the future, Erickson Associates, Inc. is committed to meeting clients' needs and strives to maintain the level of quality and integrity that was established by Ted Erickson over half a century ago.

Top photo:
*•The Westin Savannah
Harbor Resort
Just across the river from
the beauty and
heritage of Savannah...*

Center photo:
•The Club at Savannah Harbor

Lower photo:
*•Savannah International Trade
& Convention Center &
The Westin.
Basically these are 2 projects
where Erickson Associates, Inc.
completed the mechanical work.*

Kevin Barry's Irish Pub

A trip to Savannah would not be complete without a visit to the world-renowned
Kevin Barry's Irish Pub, at 117 West River Street, located on the historic riverfront.
Savannah's oldest Irish Pub opened its doors on October 31, 1980 and over
the years has garnered numerous awards for its food, drink, service, music and ambience.
It is consistently voted one of the nation's top ten Irish establishments.

Named for famed Irish Patriot and martyr, Kevin Gerard Barry, the pub focuses on patriotism and the patriotic legacies of Ireland and America.

The building itself dates from circa 1815 and houses two floors with full service bars on each and a kitchen that offers delicious food that ranges from traditional Irish fare to more modern steaks and sandwiches. A unique feature of the pub is that the kitchen serves up their mouth watering, generous dishes until 2:00 am.

The first floor dining room is home to what has been called the best showcase room in the United States. Dubbed the listening room, this smoke free venue has featured notable Irish performers over the years such as Danny Doyle, Frank Emerson, Harry O'Donoghue, Tom O'Carroll, Carroll Brown, Gabriel Donohue and Brendan Nolan. It is a universal opinion among entertainers that Kevin Barry's provides the premier platform for them to present their talents; seven nights a week.

The second floor of Kevin Barry's has been likened to a museum. Artifacts from Irish history grace the walls of the cozy Liberty Hall. The history and music has been so impressive it has helped launch the Irish Cultural Studies program at Georgia Southern University. The walls of the main room, Hall of Heroes, is an expansive and on-going tribute to the men and women of the United States Military, a Thank-you to them and their families for sacrifices made and being a part of the preservation of freedom. On top of everything else, this floor is available to meet your special needs, catered affairs from 20 to 200.

You are sure to create some wonderful memories for yourself at Kevin Barry's Pub. Put this one of a kind restaurant on your list of must see places in Savannah. You don't have to be Irish. This place is just plain rewarding all the way around.

An interior view of the cosy and charming dining room where guests are treated to southern hospitality at its best.

The Shrimp Factory

Situated on the east end of Savannah's historic River Street is one of the city's finest culinary attractions. The Shrimp Factory, opened in the summer months of 1977 by Frank and Janie Harris, is now owned by their daughter Cheryl Power. Considered a local legend in Savannah, this restaurant has become famous for its many signature recipes with Georgia Wild Shrimp, and regional Fish and Crab. Shining stars include Pine Bark Stew, Seafood Strudel, Shrimp stuffed with Deviled Crab, Seafood Bisque, Shrimp Scampi, Shrimp Jambalaya, Grouper Florentine, Pecan Flounder, Caesar Style Salad tossed tableside, Bananas Foster Flambé, and house baked Banana Bread Pudding; just to name a few.

The Shrimp Factory's building, located at 313 East River Street in the heart of the historic district, was built during the summer months of 1826, and the top floors added in the 1850's. The Savannah gray brick and Georgia heart pine beams and flooring throughout the restaurant are original. The building, originally intended as a warehouse for cotton, resin and other products being exported, is now the perfect location for dining on the Savannah River.

The perfect location for dining on the Savannah River.

Cheryl Power, The Shrimp Factory's current owner continues to ensure the flavors and consistency of her father's recipes including new additions and high service standards. In a polished yet casual and friendly atmosphere guests are treated to southern hospitality at it's finest.

We invite you to come by and have a sampling of The Shrimp Factory's signature drink, Chatham Artillery Punch, and "Watch the Ships Go By."

Open every day for Lunch until 4 pm, Dinner starts at 4 pm. Visit us online at TheShrimpFactory.com or phone 912-236-4229.

The Shrimp Factory is famous for, Pine Bark Stew, Seafood Strudel and Shrimp stuffed with Deviled Crab.

Hunter Maclean

Hunter Maclean is the premiere law firm in Savannah and represents a wide variety of companies and individuals throughout the state of Georgia, the Southeast, and the United States in legal and business matters in Georgia. The firm is headquartered in Savannah, and maintains a regional office in Brunswick, Georgia. Hunter Maclean is highly committed to its clients and the communities in which they do business.

From lower left, Robert S. Glenn, Administrative Managing Partner,
W. Brooks Stillwell, Marketing Partner and John M. Tatum, Managing Partner.

Hunter Maclean serves a clientele which includes Fortune 500 manufacturing companies, locally-based small businesses, banks, hospitals, professional service organizations, an industrial development authority, non-profit corporations, and individuals.

For more than 130 years, professionals at Hunter Maclean have been working with clients and the community as their needs have changed, their industries have expanded, and their need for legal services has evolved. Hunter Maclean is committed to focusing on its client's needs by drawing on its depth of experience and continuing to stay abreast of the industry, business and community trends that affect its clients.

With over 50 attorneys who specialize in a myriad of practice areas, Hunter Maclean offers one comprehensive source to handle the full range of each client's legal needs.

Hunter Maclean's talented attorneys have experience in a variety of practice areas including business organization, corporate governance and finance, litigation, labor and employment, bankruptcy/work-outs, estate planning/probate, immigration, insurance law, intellectual property, products liability, taxation, toxic torts, and zoning/land use.

Hunter Maclean has also developed industry specific teams in order to meet its clients' needs. These teams include hotel/hospitality, healthcare, construction, real estate (residential and development), banking, environmental, admiralty, transportation, and industrial development.

Hunter Maclean invests in the development of its professionals in response to constantly changing legal requirements and advances in technology. Hunter Maclean houses a state of

the art mediation and negotiation center, constantly upgrades its technology, and regularly hosts seminars and presentations to continue the legal education of its attorneys. These progressive attitudes and practices contribute to Hunter Maclean's ability to attract key talent as the firm continues to grow.

Hunter Maclean's philosophy of service is felt deeply in the communities in which its attorneys practice. Hunter Maclean has a tradition of providing leadership, community service, and pro bono services to local organizations. Its attorneys frequently serve on governmental boards and commissions, and are active in social service and arts organizations throughout Georgia.

Hunter Maclean is committed to serving its clients and its communities and to contributing to the long-term prosperity of both.

The Savannah Bank

Priding itself on being a "Hometown Bank," The Savannah Bank
was founded by a group of local business people who felt that the
residents of Savannah needed an independent, locally owned and operated
financial institution to meet their banking needs. The Savannah Bank
obtained a national charter and opened for business on August 22, 1990,
under the parent holding company, The Savannah Bancorp, Inc.,
a publicly traded company, with the goal of providing Savannah
and its surrounding communities with a local bank run by local faces.

Sixteen years later, 13 of the original 18 employees remain on board, as do all of the bank's original board members.

A large part of that unity is due to the bank's original mission that has remained true today - providing a bank that caters to the banking needs of the community and developing a mission statement and purpose around those needs. One step further is to have those needs constantly evaluated so to determine how well the bank is delivering its promises. From a customer, employee and shareholder's view, the real winner will always be the Savannah community.

Our vision began with the leadership of Archie H. Davis, who served as the President and Chief Executive Officer of Savannah Bancorp as well as CEO of the bank. The Savannah Bank's first decade in existence targeted small businesses and individuals leery of dealing with banks based far away. In 1996, The Savannah Bank extended its reach and launched a trust department, putting Investment Managers in place to provide clients with the ability to invest over the long term, determine goals and implement a plan to achieve them.

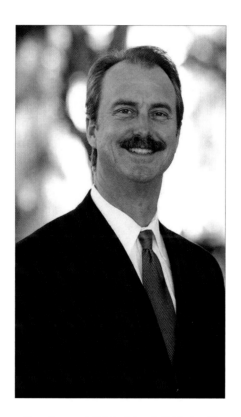

*President and CEO, John C. Helmken II
who joined the bank in 1994.*

Ground level awareness and constant assessment of the community's needs has been a predominant factor in the success of the bank, along with an internal atmosphere that encourages employees to thrive as community bankers.

The Savannah Bank, which is now led by President and CEO, John C. Helmken II, who joined the bank in 1994 and climbed the ranks until he was elected President of the bank in 2002 and CEO in 2003, also continues to hold its philosophy of corporate citizenship. The Savannah Bank is well known for its community involvement and philanthropic support in the arts and human services across Chatham County.

Today, there are more than 100 employees operating in six locations in Chatham County that offer commercial and consumer lending and deposit products, mortgage loans, as well as trust services.

The banking industry continues to become more competitive and complex, yet The Savannah Bank continues to realize that customers, day in and day out, still want the basics of courtesy, accessibility, and respect. Technology is an important tool in the evolution of business, but it is meant to act as a complement to, not in place of, the human touch.

Local Ownership. Local Decisions.
We're The Savannah Bank.

Coldwell Banker Platinum Partners

She has been in real estate for the past 33 years. She obtained her CRB (Certified Real Estate Brokerage Manager) designation in 1980, and has achieved her ABR (Accredited Buyer Representative) and CRS (Certified Relocation Specialist) designations. She was President of the Savannah Multi-List Corporation in 1990, President of the Savannah Board of Realtors in 1991, Georgia Association of Realtors Director in 1991, Georgia Association of Realtors Regional Director in 1992 and 1993, and Leadership Savannah Graduate 1994/1996 class.

She is presently Chairman of the Board of the Savannah Area Chamber of Commerce, Chairman of the Board of First National Bank, sits on the Board of Trustees for the Bethesda Home for Boys, and is a member of the Messiah Lutheran Church.

She is a loving wife, mother of two, and grandmother of six.

In her spare time she enjoys spending time with her family, cooking, boating, and is a certified scuba diver.

"Who is this?" you might ask. The bionic woman? The next Donald Trump or Richard Branson?

This is but a glimpse into the life of Connie Farmer Ray, Broker/ Owner/ Founder of Coldwell Banker Platinum Partners. Her philosophy is simple, "Stay focused on your business plan and pursue it with passion."

From St. Simons Island, Georgia to Hilton Head Island, South Carolina, the Southeastern coast has been painted blue by Coldwell Banker Platinum Partners. Coldwell Banker Platinum Partners, with its nine office locations spanning Beaufort County, Chatham County, Effingham County, Bryan County, and Glynn County, has formed a tight bond. This synergy of offices allows for seamless service of the real estate needs of anyone looking for a home or property in Southeast Georgia and the South Carolina Lowcountry.

Locally owned and operated by Connie Farmer Ray, Coldwell Banker Platinum Partners has grown into a market leader that prides itself in Southern hospitality and real estate professionalism. Since the opening of its first office in the spring of 1995, Coldwell Banker Platinum Partners has grown to nine offices with more than 170 sales associates, a fully staffed relocation department, new construction site sales, property management services, and residential and commercial sales.

Coldwell Banker Platinum Partners

Connie Farmer Ray

operates on the belief that "with our wide range of resources, we now have the unique opportunity to provide more services to our customers," says Ms. Ray. Because of their commitment to professionalism and personalized service (the core of their business philosophy) Coldwell Banker Platinum Partners has excelled in the face of competition. According to Real Trends Magazine,

Coldwell Banker Platinum Partners is one of the top 500 real estate companies nationally, and one of the top 100 Coldwell Banker affiliates worldwide for the fifth straight year. The Cendant Corporation has awarded Coldwell Banker Platinum Partners with the Cendant Mobility 5 Star Circle of Excellence Award.

Coldwell Banker Platinum Partners continues to stay cutting edge by researching new ideas on increasing the services offered to its clients and customers. "One stop shopping is the future of our company. We will continue to offer services, technology, and most importantly a personal touch in every facet of our clients' and customers' real estate needs," says Connie Farmer Ray. It is in this process that Coldwell Banker Platinum Partners is more than just a Realtor. From searching for the perfect home to applying for a loan and even to moving in, Coldwell Banker Platinum Partners makes finding the right home for you a quick, easy, and pleasurable experience for anyone looking for a home or property along the Georgia and South Carolina coasts.

There is an unmistakable inviting warmth and unique Southern charm that leads many of us to call Savannah home. It is in this great tradition that Coldwell Banker Platinum Partners prides itself on helping find the perfect home for each of its clients, leaving them with what's right, not what's left.

Boar's Head Grill & Tavern

Towering above a centuries-old ballastone pathway, Boar's Head Grill & Tavern, located at 1 North Lincoln Street Ramp at East River, offers an unusual blend of fine dining, historical importance, as well as a ghostly tale or two. One of the finest examples of eighteenth and nineteenth century architecture, this former cotton warehouse was constructed in 1780 and helped establish Savannah as one of the world's largest headquarters for the cotton trade.

Incidentally, there is said to be a leftover relic from that time - the spirit of 19-year-old former female slave who frequents the dwelling today, playfully calling out employees' names, blowing out candles, turning on water faucets and the like.

Legend also has it that this unique warehouse sits above the stomping ground of the notoriously treacherous 18th century pirate, Edward Teach, also known as Blackbeard, who terrorized the wealthy merchants of the Savannah River that sits below.

Yet, local owners Philip and Charlene Branan, who are both from Savannah and bought the establishment together in 1998, assure locals and tourists alike that they will walk away with more than just a fantastic experience - they will in fact, partake in a one-of-a-kind authentic, culinary treat.

Offering casual, riverfront dining in a tavern setting with evenings set by candlelight and lunches with good cheer, Boar's Head was established in 1964, claiming its stature as the first restaurant on River Street, as well as being one of the earliest conversions along the entire riverfront.

Long-known as a local favorite, this institution has acted as a host to numerous special occasions over the years for locals and stationed military men at nearby Fort Stewart, and continues to cater to the infinitely growing stream of tourists on a regular basis. To this day, the restaurant warrants many nostalgic memories for those who celebrated their first dates, anniversaries and birthdays at the riverfront hotspot.

It was for that same reason that the Branans, who were longtime patrons of the restaurant themselves, decided not to change the name of this significant landmark.

Instead, they tweaked the menu and made a few cosmetic changes, but were careful to preserve the original, exposed ballastones, bricks and other architectural details while carefully restoring the Heart of Pine floors. And in an effort to make customers feel even more welcome, the kitchen walls were taken down so that owner Chef Philip could converse with guests. A graduate of the famed Culinary Institute of America, Chef Philip offers variety for the more sophisticated palette, as well as those seeking traditional southern fare. Specialties include Savannah "She" Crab Soup, Black-Eyed Pea & Ham Soup with Collard Greens, Oysters Rockefeller, Barbequed Shrimp, Low Country Bouillabaisse, Filet Mignon, Maine Lobster, Stuffed Grouper, Chef Philip's Famous Crabcakes and his Award-Winning Chocolate Bread Pudding.

Chef?Owner Philip Branan
CIA Graduate 1984

Home made Desserts
Savannah Trifle
Creme Brulee with
Raspberry Sauce
White Chocolate Cheesecake with
Raspberry Sauce
Jack Daniels Chocolate Pecan Pie
Flourless Chocolate Torte
Key Lime Pie

J.T. Turner Construction Co., Inc.

High quality craftsmanship and service have secured J.T. Turner Construction Co., Inc. as one of Savannah's most reputable full service general contractors. The Company is licensed to build in Georgia, South Carolina, and Florida. J.T. Turner Construction Co., Inc. specializes in the following areas: Custom Homes, Historic Preservation, Commercial and Industrial Facilities, Remodeling, Insurance Repair, and Commercial Tenant Build Out. Examples of the Company's work can be found throughout downtown Savannah, Tybee Island, The Landings at Skidaway Island, Dutch Island, Marsh Harbor, Southbridge, Commodore Point, The Yacht Club Estates, Yellow Bluff, The Ford Plantation, and Palmetto Bluff.

J.T. Turner, Jr., the sole shareholder of the Company, grew up in Thomasville, Georgia and graduated from Mercer University in Macon, Georgia. Prior to moving to Savannah, he pursued all aspects of the building and restoration business by working for several construction and restoration contractors. He learned the financial aspects of the business while working at a bank in Macon. In 1976, on the advice of friend and local businessman Hugh Armstrong, Sr., Jim started the company known today as J.T. Turner Construction, Co., Inc.

The organization of the Company includes seasoned project managers who estimate and supervise projects. The Company also employs a full-time estimating staff for additional support in preparing bids for large projects. The Company achieves a high level of quality at competitive prices by constantly adding to its large pool of subcontractors. The field staff is comprised of superintendents, job foremen, carpenters and apprentices.

J.T. Turner, Jr. is joined by his son and daughter, both who are employed by the company: (l/r) Mischa Turner, J.T. Turner, Jr., and J.T. Turner, III (Tripp).

Mr. Turner is a goal setter with high expectations of success for the staff and the Company. He demands excellence and leadership from his personnel in every phase of the business. He has assembled professionals with the requisite experience and knowledge to enable the Company to maintain its position as a leader in the industry. Budgeting, planning, quality control and client follow-up are routine responsibilities for all members of his staff. Mr. Turner is a believer in the value of both long-term and short-term business plans. He has ambitious plans for the Company including the continued success of its employees.

J.T. Turner Construction Co., Inc. has received multiple awards noting its workmanship. The Company has been honored to receive many awards from the Georgia Trust for Historic Preservation, Inc. and the Historic Savannah Foundation. Restored projects include Nationally Registered Properties and National Historic Landmarks, such as the King-Tisdell Cottage, Owens-Thomas House Museum, and Isle of Hope United Methodist Church.

The Company has been noted in key publications such as Coastal Living, House Beautiful, Custom Builder, Savannah Magazine, Southern Accents, Leading Estates of the World, Home, Professional Builder, and Architectural Digest. The Company has also enjoyed televised attention with projects being showcased on Homes Across America, Savannah: Death and Rebirth of a City, and Give Me Shelter. In addition, Turner Construction also had the privilege of being chosen to appear in the weekly televised program of This Old House.

J.T. Turner Construction Co., Inc. is committed to maintaining the highest level of quality performance and excellence in service. The clients of J.T. Turner Construction Co., Inc. can trust that they will receive nothing less than quality performance and a solid, successful finished product.

Featured here is one of J.T. Turner Construction Co., Inc's commercial projects: First Chatham Bank, Hodgson Memorial Branch. Turner Construction has built five branches for First Chatham Bank, with plans to build a sixth in the very near future.

Georgia Power

In July 2006, after 124 years of proud service to the Savannah area, Savannah Electric completed its merger into Georgia Power. Both subsidiaries of Southern Company, this merger came 18 years after Savannah Electric joined the system through an earlier merger.

Georgia Power's top priority is customer service. This means keeping reliability high and electric rates low. The company has won national awards for customer satisfaction – a key component of its overall business strategy. Georgia Power ranks in the top quartile among peer utilities in customer satisfaction surveys.

Georgia Power has a strong tradition of community service, powering Georgia's progress for more than a century. Preston Arkwright, Georgia Power's first president, gave the company its first motto, "A Citizen Wherever We Serve." It is a vision that still guides the way for Georgia Power people.

Georgia Power's 9,000 employees play important roles in the communities throughout the state. They can be found volunteering for charities and service organizations and supporting local civic groups statewide.

Highly skilled employees and investment in state-of-the-art equipment result in reliable service that customers count on.

In addition to contributions to qualifying non-profit agencies, the company provides talent and other resources across the state to the many community projects it supports. Georgia Power focuses its involvement to improve education, protect the environment, support health and human services and sustain diversity initiatives.

As Southern Company's largest subsidiary, the company serves more than 2.2 million customers in all but four of Georgia's 159 counties. Its 132 business offices ensure a statewide presence for the investor-owned utility.

Georgia Power receives numerous awards for its contributions to the state's economic development. In 2005, Georgia Power played a key role in bringing $1.4 billion in new capital investment projects and more than 8,900 new jobs into the state. That same year, *Site Selection* magazine

ranked Georgia Power's Community and Economic Development organization one of the best in the world for the seventh year in a row.

The company's competitive electricity prices help Georgia maintain its position as one of the fastest-growing states in the nation and the Savannah area as a shining economic star. To energize that growth, the company continues to invest about a billion dollars a year in electric infrastructure, bringing its total investment in facilities to $20.4 billion.

Through that investment, paired with the dedicated efforts of employees, Georgia Power will keep up with rising electricity demand and maintain the high level of electric reliability that customers expect and deserve.

When storms cause trouble, Georgia Power crews respond to restore power quickly and safely.

Company employees take great pride in their skills; in fact they're among the world's best. Georgia Power line crews (including Savannah teams) frequently take top positions in the International Lineman's Rodeo competition.

Savannah College of Art and Design

Dream big; make a difference

The idea of starting a brand new art college in Savannah, Georgia, may have seemed ridiculous in 1978, but in 2006 it is hard to imagine what Savannah would have been like without "SCAD." The founders of the Savannah College of Art and Design had vision, and some say a lot of chutzpah, but they never imagined that in just 26 years their idea would flourish to encompass 7,500 students, 10,000 alumni, three campuses and virtual classrooms via the Internet.
They just wanted to make a difference in the lives of aspiring artists.

Starting with the circa 1892 Savannah Volunteer Guards Armory at 342 Bull St. to house SCAD's first classrooms, studios, library and offices, founders President Paula Wallace, Richard Rowan, May Poetter and Paul Poetter kept students as the focus and quality as the goal. Through imagination, determination and hard work, they created and guided the growth of an institution of stature in academia while building a campus through renovation and adaptive reuse of significant historic structures.

The SCAD curriculum is solid, yet innovative, including foundation studies and liberal arts as the basis of each major program. The mission is focused: The Savannah College of Art and Design exists to prepare talented students for careers, emphasizing learning through individual attention in a positively oriented environment.

At SCAD, the unique qualities of each student are nurtured through an interesting curriculum, in an inspiring environment, under the leadership of involved professors. Students have access to more than 3,000 computer workstations configured with high-end software used throughout the art and design professions. In addition, students work on specialized equipment such as a Computer Numeric Controlled milling machine, Titan rapid 3-D printer system, Steadicam EFP, Sony High Definition cameras and Digidesign Pro Tools audio workstations. Even the fibers department has AVL Compu-Dobby looms and an AVL electronic jacquard handloom.

SCAD faculty possess excellent credentials and relevant experience that translate into networking opportunities for students. SCAD graduates are in demand with such firms as Digital Domain, Pixar, the Cartoon Network, ILM, Sony Imageworks, Heery International, Hirsch Bedner Associates, Nike, American Greetings, Turner Studios, The Weather Channel, MTV, CNN,

Bill Blass, Saks Fifth Avenue, Bisou Bisou, American Eagle Outfitters, Phat Farm, Target, Anthropologie, Esprit, the National Football League, Gulfstream Aerospace, Procter & Gamble, Samsung, BMW DesignWorks and Disney Imagineering, among countless others.

Signature events created and sponsored by SCAD include the Savannah Film Festival, the International Festival, the spring Fashion Show, the Sidewalk Arts Festival, the Sand Arts Festival and the Game Developers Exchange. The college calendar also includes lectures, plays, concerts, and exhibitions by renowned artists and designers.

What began as an interesting idea in 1978 is now a highly regarded institution of higher learning. Campuses in Lacoste, France, and Atlanta, Georgia, now add a medieval French village and a major metropolitan hub to the mix. And students can log on to SCAD e-Learning from anywhere in the world.

SCAD provides an education that equips graduates to make enriching contributions to life and to society. Perhaps this is why the editors of Kaplan/Newsweek's 2006 guide to America's Hottest Colleges chose SCAD as the Hottest for Studying Art among "America's 25 Hottest Colleges." The message is clear: Dream big; you can make a difference.

EMC Engineering Services, Inc.

Founded by Larry M. Stuber in 1978, EMC Engineering Services, Inc. (EMC) began as a one-man operation that initially provided clients with planning and design services in the environmental, marine and civil engineering fields.

However, with strong leadership and a solid reputation for high quality, cost effective projects, and emphasis on employees' individual and team growth, the firm had tripled in size by 1982. The office moved from its original offices on Liberty Street to its present location at 23 East Charlton Street, in the heart of the downtown historic business district. EMC's office building was in the opening scene of the movie "Forest Gump". In 1985, as the firm continued to expand, the entire building was acquired, further establishing its prominent role in local business.

Since that time, EMC has diversified into many other areas, including wetlands mitigation, landscape architecture, land surveying, hydrographic surveying, Geographic Information Systems, construction management, and flood reduction and mitigation making it a leading southeastern consulting engineering firm.

EMC is able to offer its wide range of services to municipalities, governmental agencies, industries and businesses in the Southeastern United States due to its structure, as well as its placement of strategically located offices. There are production branches in Statesboro, Brunswick, Albany, Augusta, Valdosta, Columbus and Atlanta, Georgia and project administration offices in Glennville, Georgia, Mobile, Alabama and Panama City, Florida.

EMC offers expertise in four divisions including Construction Engineering Inspection, Site Development Engineering, Survey, and infrastructure. Each division further consists of specialized departments to provide more responsive and efficient service to clients. Those services include transportation, recreational planning, drainage, surveying, wetlands delineation, site development, materials testing and golf course design, among many others.

Each project is supervised by a manager who is responsible for meeting the client's specific needs. And to further

Savannah College Of Art & Design Boundary Village.

Derenne Avenue Stormwater Pumping Station.

support the various production departments, all owners are actively engaged in managing projects based on their particular expertise.

As an employee-owned company, EMC's employees are encouraged to work towards shared ownership of the company, creating professional well-being through individual and team development and profit.

It is this ownership philosophy that has allowed the company to achieve continuity within key positions at EMC, resulting in the development of long-term client and engineer relationships that are so important to any service organization.

EMC employs a staff of more than 175 professional engineers, construction inspectors, scientists, technicians and surveyors.

The firm has an outstanding record of growth, expansion and providing quality services to its clients, which is the direct outcome of individual efforts and close cooperation by all of its staff members. EMC's future success depends upon the continuation of these efforts, adherence to the highest professional standards and ideals and the ongoing commitment to satisfying the client's needs by using state-of-the-art technology and equipment.

National Office Systems

Savannah's most successful and innovative companies rely on National Office Systems, Inc. (natoffsys.com) to design, finish, and furnish their commercial, healthcare, and learning facilities. With highly trained professionals who understand the complexities and intricate nature of design, as well as the importance of strong customer service, NOS ranks as Savannah's leading full-service contract furnishings and interior design firm.

First established as a Herman Miller (hermanmiller.com) dealership in Savannah on State and Jefferson streets more than 22 years ago, Scott Center, a Savannah native, took over the business five years later, to become president and CEO. Today the business stands at 125 Martin Luther King Boulevard and flourishes as an open, cutting-edge interior design resource.

Armed with technologically advanced products and services of the highest quality, NOS showcases over 200 lines of furniture and serves as the exclusive Herman Miller dealer in coastal Georgia and South Carolina. A leader in technology, environmental design, and ergonomics, Herman Miller is widely known as the manufacturer of the Aeron Chair. No other chair, despite numerous attempts to imitate, has been found to be as comfortable, supportive, and ergonomically correct. NOS is also the exclusive DIRTT Environmental Wall Dealer (dirtt.net) in the region. DIRTT is the next generation completely movable full height wall. DIRTT walls are beautiful, technologically advanced, environmentally friendly, and depreciates over 7 years, as opposed to 39 years for standard drywall construction.

The designers/project managers at NOS are able to use their well-versed knowledge of the products and of the clientele to create the perfect work environment that fits within the client's budget. Their ultimate goal is to create interior comfort, safety and efficiency, in tandem with proper work flow, ergonomics, local codes, and environmental design. Scott Center is a LEED™ accredited professional.

Staff members are also unique in that they will oversee every aspect of a job down to the carpeting, tile, window treatments, wall coverings, painting, light construction, art and accessories.

Attention to such detail is what has allowed NOS to provide most of the innovative, cutting-edge interiors in the region to such clients as JCB, Lummus, Cora Bett Thomas Realty Company, the Savannah/Hilton Head International Airport, the Savannah Economic Development Authority, and the Telfair Museum of Art's new Jepson Center for Fine Arts.

NOS has also become the leading choice for our area's most progressive educators. The Live Oak Library Systems in Savannah, The Savannah Technical College, South University, Georgia Southern University, and Armstrong Atlantic State University are only a few who have called upon the talents of NOS to create state-of-the-art environments for their campuses.

However, the firm is not limited to the technologically-savvy. It also caters to the most traditional interior spaces, working with ergonomic features that can be seamlessly incorporated into conservative, high quality furnishings.

Savannah's wealth managers, attorneys, medical and insurance offices also rely on the firm. Clients include Oliver Maner & Gray LLP, The Savannah Bank, First Chatham Bank, Regions Bank, and Palmer & Cay, for both local and national offices, among many others.

OLIVER MANER & GRAY LLP

Founded in 1897 as Twiggs & Oliver, Oliver Maner & Gray LLP has grown from a small firm comprised of a handful of excellent attorneys to its current twenty-five attorneys with a broad based practice area which spans the State of Georgia and beyond. The firm has focused on quality growth by adding experienced lawyers with strong reputations and by grooming the next generation of lawyers in house.

Tom Gray and Jim Pannell are both nationally recognized bond counsel with experience in hundreds of governmental and private activity bonds. They have each represented issuers throughout the State of Georgia, and have obtained financing in excess of ten billion dollars.

"Vigorous representation" is how Greg Hodges describes the philosophy of OMG's trial practice, a description that can be verified by clients, judges and opposing counsel. Hodges and his partner Bill Franklin are consistently honored by their peers as being among the best in the State and the nation and have built a medical malpractice defense practice of unparalleled standing.

In another practice area, Pat O'Connor has developed one of the most sought after municipal liability defense practices in the state and has also been extremely successful defending fellow lawyers in legal malpractice actions. In recent years, O'Connor has also established himself as one of the most highly regarded and respected mediators in the area.

Tim Roberts and Chris Ray are two young partners who have used their early experience as defense lawyers to develop their own practice in those areas while also branching out into commercial litigation, business disputes and serious personal injury and wrongful death actions. Similarly, Patty Paul's years of experience working with other partners on workers compensation and other complex litigation matters have helped develop her expertise in discovery matters, employment litigation and appellate practice.

Partners David Dickey, Bob Schivera and Lee Summerford combine with Julian Friedman, who is Of Counsel to the firm, to form OMG's Tax and Corporate Department - a practice as broad as the name implies. This department has vast experience in dealing with probate issues, drafting wills and trusts and implementing complex tax-motivated estate planning. These partners also focus on the formation

and representation of corporations, partnerships and LLCs, with a particular emphasis on the legal and health care issues affecting physicians and group practices.

Jim Gerard and Marvin Fentress lead the Real Estate Department focusing on commercial real estate and development and complex financial transactions, but they are also members of a rare breed of general practitioners with broad areas of practice from litigation to creditors rights to general representation of large interstate businesses. Gerard also has decades of experience representing small municipalities which makes him a valuable resource in the area of municipal law.

OMG's reputation has been earned by attorneys who share a philosophy rooted in excellence, loyalty to clients and hard work. In the words of managing partner Pat O'Connor, "Oliver Maner & Gray LLP is not one of the biggest or flashiest law firms in Georgia, just one of the best."

Savannah Technical College

Savannah Technical College has been meeting the needs of its community for 75 years, as the area's leading provider of high-quality, industry-driven technical education. After five years of explosive growth in enrollment, the College now serves 4,000 students each quarter in Bryan, Chatham, Effingham and Liberty Counties, offering more than 50 certificate, diploma and associate degree programs in allied health, business and applied manufacturing.

Working closely with business and community partners, the College develops programs designed to meet the changing needs of the regional economy with the flexibility and creativity necessary to sustain the workforce of the future. The College demonstrates its commitment to workforce development by partnering with employers to deliver programs off-site in area hospitals, specially-equipped community education centers and public high schools, making it easier for students of all ages to acquire new skills and improve their lives.

It is a time of enthusiastic growth and expansion for Savannah Technical College. New instructional programs in healthcare, business and applied manufacturing provide students with the career education necessary to compete in today's economy. Our hospitality program will boast its first graduating class this year - making employment and career advancement in today's fast-paced tourism industry a reality. New programs in management and paralegal studies compliment successful programs in accounting, computing and marketing. Practical nursing remains a top choice for many prospective students seeking healthcare careers. The medical and dental assisting programs produce certified graduates for area practitioners. In industry, short-term certificate programs place graduates in industries ranging from HVAC to manufacturing, electrical and automotive. The Savannah Campus boasts a newly-opened state-of-the-art service center for students, new laboratory spaces, an expanded learning enrichment center and multi-purpose learning center. A $20 million Center for Allied Health Sciences and Learning Success is planned to support continued enrollment growth.

With the opening of the Army Education Center on Fort Stewart, the College has a presence on post to serve military families with the skills and education they need for success. The Liberty Campus continues to serve the educational needs of the community with programs in nursing, early childhood education, computers and technology. The Crossroads Technology Campus, a key element in the development of a high-tech corridor along I-95, is a catalyst for regional business development. Construction is under way on a campus to serve the growing communities in Effingham County.

Through its commitment to quality, service and responiveness to its community, the College remains an intengral force in the growth and development of southeast Georgia. Savannah Technical College is accredited by the Southern Association of Colleges and Schools to award the associate degree.

Celia Dunn
Sotheby's International Realty
A tradition of integrity

Savannah is unlike any other city on earth; not surprisingly, its real estate market is unlike any other as well. Whether searching for that dream home, selling an existing home or exploring the possibilities of commercial property, the knowledge and experience harbored by Celia Dunn Sotheby's International Realty can be invaluable in today's competitive market. The brokers at Celia Dunn Sotheby's International Realty are home-grown specialists. They've spent a lifetime exploring the city's streets, getting to know its many moods and pursuing its expanding horizons. They know Savannah.

Celia Dunn Sotheby's International Realty was founded by Celia W. Dunn 25 years ago. Her husband, J. Laurence Dunn, joined her in the company shortly thereafter. The Dunns had established themselves as leaders on Savannah's competitive real estate scene before opening the doors of their own office, now comfortably ensconced at 9 - 13 - 17 West Charlton Street on Madison Square in the center of Savannah's Historic District;

*Celia Dunn the founder of
Celia Dunn Sotheby's International Realty.*

with a second office located at 6 Bruin Street in Bluffton, South Carolina.

Backed by years of experience and a passion for Savannah, Celia Dunn built a successful business on the philosophy of community involvement and unfailing professional integrity. Her business acumen and personal commitment continue to attract an outstanding staff of real estate professionals who are actively involved in civic and cultural ventures throughout the city and are eager to acquaint prospective home buyers with the best Savannah has to offer.

Celia Dunn Sotheby's International Realty specializes in fine luxury residential and commercial properties throughout coastal Georgia and the South Carolina Low Country. From premier Historic District and Ardsley Park listings to exclusive waterfront homes, large tracts of land and choice developments, the company's agents strive to help clients locate that perfect property. In addition to outstanding customer service, the company has earned a reputation for its local expertise and the strength of its property management department.

In recent years, Savannah and the Low Country of South Carolina have seen tremendous change and growth. Selling a home, a commercial property, land, or development can be more exciting — and challenging – as a result. The professionals at Celia Dunn Sotheby's International Realty develop customized marketing and targeted advertising to guide real estate sales. Traditional tools, such as the Multiple Listing Service, open houses and promotional events, as well as the latest electronic media are utilized to maximize exposure. The Sotheby's website and network are invaluable to sales and unique to this company.

Our group of agents, representing a rich variety of talent, backgrounds and interests, reflects the ever growing diversity of Savannah's charming neighborhoods and gracious communities as well as coastal Georgia and the South Carolina Low Country. Together, with the firm's managing brokers, they are committed to their neighbors and their community and are dedicated to providing caring, personalized service to their clients.

Celia Dunn Sotheby's International Realty's outstanding staff of real estate professionals.

Yates-Astro Termite and Pest Control

Savannah's gracious homes and historic buildings attract more than tourists. With our unique coastal ecosystem, Georgia leads the nation in the incidence of termite damage to residential property. Subterranean termites represent a greater threat to property in Savannah than tornadoes, fire, and hurricanes combined.

Since 1928, Yates-Astro Termite and Pest Control has been helping local homeowners and businesses protect their property from serious threats posed by termites and other pests. Originally founded by F.H. Yates, the company is among the oldest pest control services in the nation. With a team of 100 employees, Yates-Astro is the largest independent pest control company in southeast Georgia with branches in Hinesville, Statesboro, and Brunswick and sister companies servicing Hilton Head Island, Valdosta, Tifton, Thomasville, and Moultrie.

In addition to attracting termites, Savannah's climate also provides an ideal breeding ground for ants, roaches, rats, fleas and many other nuisance pests. With the goal of eliminating problematic pests before they appear, Yates-Astro offers a variety of preventative treatment programs. For pest control, bimonthly, monthly, quarterly, and annual treatment programs are available to fit the specific needs of each customer. Experience has shown the bimonthly treatment program to be especially effective in our low country environment.

The Face of Yates - Astro
The homeless roach singing the "Cockroach Blues" has been made famous on television, radio, and in print. As long as Yates-Astro is around, he'll continue to sing the cockroach blues.

locally owned company. For commercial customers with reputations to maintain, customers to impress, and property to protect, Yates-Astro provides a customized systems approach. Yates-Astro serves the majority of the area's finest hotels, restaurants, retail facilities, hospitals, office buildings, and manufacturing facilities.

Locally owned and operated by the Culbreth family since 1975, Yates-Astro provides a unique level of service to the community that provides an edge over national competitors in meeting the needs of individual customers. A priority is placed on purchasing supplies locally, and the Yates-Astro family of employees is active in the Savannah Rotary Club, Southside Rotary, Executive Association of Savannah, Chamber of Commerce,

The Yates - Astro Management Team
L to R: Jimmy Cannon, Mike Hobbs, Chuck Thompson, Mark Willmon, Rick Culbreth, Mary Ellen Trainor, and Brian Loomis.

No Job Is Too Large
With one hundred employees Yates-Astro's staff has the expertise and the equipment to handle any job.

One of Yates-Astro's greatest strengths is its termite warranty program which is regarded as among the best in the industry. The warranty is solid, and the company is large enough to stand behind it. The real competitive advantage, however, springs from the company's local ownership. If retreatment is needed or if repairs from termite damage become necessary, customers contact the local office which provides a prompt response only available when dealing with a

Homebuilders Association of Savannah, Tourism Leadership Council, and the Savannah Area BUY LOCAL Committee. Yates-Astro also maintains membership in the Georgia Pest Control Association and National Pest Management Association. With a long history of remarkable service and its commitment to the community, Yates-Astro Termite and Pest Control leads the industry in protecting thousands of homes and businesses in Savannah and the surrounding areas.

International Paper

The Savannah Paper Mill opened in 1935 when the first paper machine was installed. That was the beginning of a long-term relationship between the mill and the seaside city of Savannah. The facility has grown since that time to one of the largest manufacturing sites in International Paper. Over one billion dollars of capital has been invested at the site in the past two decades.

The Savannah Mill is located on a 450-acre site on the Savannah River that includes three International Paper manufacturing facilities and a nine hole public golf course which is owned by the mill.

The Savannah Paper Mill employs 650 people who work making pulp and paper. Our 520 hourly employees are represented by five unions: the United Steel Workers; the International Association of Machinists and Aerospace Workers; the International Brotherhood of Electrical Workers, the United Association of Journeymen and Apprentices of the Plumbing and Pipefitting Industry of the United States and Canada; and the International Brotherhood of Boilermakers, Iron Shipbuilders, Blacksmiths, Forgers and Helpers of America.

The Savannah Mill produces rolls of paper that are converted at facilities around the world. Our operations include a woodyard, pulp mill, power boiler, turbines that generate electricity, a chemical recovery process, and three paper machines. Forty percent of the products made at Savannah are exported to Europe, Asia, South America, and China though the Georgia ports.

Companies around the world depend on the products made at the Savannah Mill. Paper made at the mill is sent to their converting plants and turned into packaging for everything from computers to washing machines to agricultural products. Laminated countertops and panels, made using our paper, are installed in homes around the world.

International Paper also operates other businesses on the Savannah site. Along with a corrugated container plant that produces boxes for use in industry and agriculture, Arizona Chemical operates a manufacturing plant, research facility and a manufacturing plant joint venture with the Chilean Arboris, LLC on the site. Arizona Chemical is a company of IP and is a leading producer of high-value pine chemicals for the adhesives, inks and coatings, and oleochemical markets.

Making paper isn't the only important thing at the Savannah mill. The mill and its employees are also concerned about making a positive impact on their community. Over the years the International Paper employees have invested thousands of hours of service in the Savannah community and donated literally millions of dollars to the community. International Paper employees are active in groups such as The Savannah Chamber of Commerce, the Junior Achievement Society, the Boy Scouts, Senior Citizens, American Red Cross, local schools and church sponsored programs, and volunteer fire departments.

For the past seventy years the Savannah Mill has called Savannah home. The International Paper businesses on the Savannah site today are proud to be a part of this dynamic, successful community.

Georgia Eye Institute: Establishing Excellence in Eye Care

The physicians of the Georgia Eye Institute
Front Row (left to right): Elizabeth Miller, M.D., Sanford Rosenthal, M.D., Allan Wexler, O.D., Matthew Deich, M.D., David Kim, M.D., John DeVaro, M.D.
Back Row (left to right): James Beisel, O.D., J.C. Parker, O.D., Christopher Hinson, O.D., Michael Landa, M.D., William Degenhart, M.D., Joseph Gussler, M.D.,
Kerry Freeman, M.D. (Not pictured: Joseph Stubbs, M.D., and Thomas Dunham, O.D.)

When William Degenhart, M.D., left private practice in the early 1990s to run a multi-specialty eye institute in Savannah, he had one goal in mind: To provide excellence in eye care. Today, that still holds true for the Georgia Eye Institute. As the only multi-specialty eye facility in the area, Georgia Eye offers a comprehensive scope of services from general ophthalmology to ocular trauma.

The model for Georgia Eye Institute - one eye center that houses both general ophthalmologists and a variety of sub-specialists - was based on the renowned Wills Eye Hospital in Philadelphia. The ability to refer patients to a sub-specialist who is in-house is one of the things that makes Georgia Eye Institute unique.

"What makes us special is that everyone is under one roof and it's a seamless system," said Degenhart. "If someone comes in with blurred vision and it's a retina problem, we can take the patient upstairs and they can immediately see a retina specialist."

The physicians at Georgia Eye Institute provide sub-specialty services in pediatric ophthalmology, cataract, glaucoma, refractive technology, cornea, ocular plastics, lacrimal, ocular trauma, orbital, retina, and vitreous. The immediate, face-to-face consultations with Georgia Eye Institute physicians not only enhances patient care, but also ensures efficient patient flow and management.

In addition to personal, specialized service, Georgia Eye Institute is also known for staying on the leading edge of technology in eye care. Some of the procedures available at Georgia Eye include, Conductive Keratoplasty for improvement of presbyopia, optical coherence tomography, digital retinal photography, and Wavefront technology for refractive surgical procedures.

Georgia Eye has a fully equipped outpatient surgery suite for minor procedures and a convenient optical dispensary

with a wide variety of frame styles and options. Georgia Eye is located on the campus of Memorial Health University Medical Center (MHUMC), which means the physicians of Georgia Eye have access to all of the patient care services offered by MHUMC. As part of the affiliation with MHUMC, the only teaching and research hospital in the Southeast, the Georgia Eye physicians participate in educating medical residents.

The main office of Georgia Eye is located in Savannah; however, satellite locations can also be found in Claxton, Richmond Hill, Rincon, Springfield, Statesboro, and Vidalia. And while Georgia Eye Institute has grown since its beginnings more than a decade ago, a commitment to excellence in eye care still remains the focus of the physicians and staff that take care of patients every day.

"We're here to provide comprehensive eye care," said Degenhart. "And that's what we do."

Brasseler USA

Headquartered in Savannah since 1980, Brasseler USA is a leading instrumentation and power systems provider to healthcare professionals in the Dental, Orthopedic, Neurosurgery, ENT, Oral Maxiofacial surgery, Podiatry and Cosmetic surgery markets. Brasseler USA products are trusted and employed daily in dental, hospital and surgi-center operatories across North America and around the world.

Brasseler USA was originally founded in Chicago, IL in 1976 by Peter Brasseler II. Mr. Brasseler moved the facility to Savannah based on the availability of a strong, skilled labor force, developed highways and port facilities, an international airport and climate ideal for year-round production. Brasseler USA's 85,000 square foot Savannah complex includes Administration, Sales & Marketing, Finance, Customer Service, IT, Manufacturing and Distribution facilities housed in two buildings.

Don Waters, Brasseler USA President and Chief Executive Officer and a Savannah native, ensures that although the company conducts business around the globe, it doesn't fail to fulfill its responsibility to the Savannah area. Thecompany actively supports many local charities including the United Way, the American Cancer Society, local hospitals, and Union Mission, among others. "Brasseler USA is proud to be an active corporate member of the Savannah community. We're proud of Savannah's rich cultural heritage, and very pleased to be a part of this dynamic and growing city. We take very seriously our commitment to our customers around the world; however, we also strongly believe we have a responsibility to our Savannah-based employees and their families, and to the greater local community. This orientation is core to the corporate creed and values at Brasseler USA."

The dental business segment of Brasseler USA has long been the market leader in dental rotary cutting instruments. In the past few years, however, it has expanded its product assortment to include a full line of Preventative Care and Endodontic instrument offerings. In 2004, Brasseler USA entered into a partnership in North America with one of the world's leading manufacturers of air and electric power systems, NSK Nakanishi, Inc. of Tochigi-ken, Japan, to market and distribute power systems under a Brasseler/NSK co-brand. The result of this recent expansion is that Brasseler USA's dental business, with over 350 catalog pages of product, is the single largest branded provider of dental instrumentation in North America.

In 1987, Brasseler USA entered the medical instrument market with the creation of Komet Medical Surgical Power Accessories. Marketed today under the Brasseler brand in North America and the Tava brand internationally, the medical line of products features a line of surgical power accessories, including rotary cutters and surgical saw blades for use by orthopedic surgeons, neurosurgeons, ENT surgeons, cardio-vascular surgeons and other physicians. Brasseler Medical also manufactures and markets a complete line of small and large bone surgical power systems across its segments, and is a leader in surgical power systems repair.

With a strong product line and brand name, and firmly entrenched in large, growing healthcare markets, Brasseler USA is positioned for continued solid growth well into the future.

The Savannah Pilots Association

The Savannah Pilots Association, one of the nation's oldest, has always played an important role in the growth and development of Savannah's ports and economy, as well as the state of Georgia's economic well-being. From the early days of commerce in the United States to modern day, the Savannah Pilots Association has safely guided vessels on the 25.5 mile journey from the sea into the port of Savannah, which was recently named the fourth busiest facility in the United States. An estimated 2,002,500 containers will pass through the port by year's end, which would be an increase of more than half a million containers from the 2005 fiscal year. Much of this is due to Savannah's increasingly strong share of the lucrative Asian market, holding at 15.3 percent, second only to the Port of New York/New Jersey.

There have been many milestones and historic events that have contributed to making the Savannah ports an international transportation hub, but one of the most integral components of the port's success has been the professionalism and dedication of the members of the Savannah Pilots Association.

The profession of American pilotage began in 1789 when the First Congress of the United States recognized the occupation, and under the Commerce Clause of the Constitution drafted legislation leaving state pilotage under the direction of the individual states. Savannah's international trade, however, was launched 40 years earlier when James Habersham and Charles Harris formed an export/import company and sent the first commercial vessel to England loaded with deer skins, lumber, and livestock valued at $10,000. Prior to this venture, all international trade in and out of Savannah had to pass through Port Royal or Charleston, South Carolina.

By the beginning of the 1800s, international trade between Savannah and England had reached $2 million annually and more and more capable pilots were needed to guide the ships through the muddy waters of the Savannah River channel. At that time, the river was only 10 feet deep, but even then the pilots took advantage of tidal increases of several feet to maneuver larger vessels into port.

In April 1864, the city of Atlanta fell beneath the onslaught of General Sherman's Army and in the following

months the Union Army began its march to the sea. During this chaotic time a group of far-sighted state pilots met to formally organize, and thus began the Savannah Pilots Association. Aware that Savannah's port was certain to grow and develop after the war, these men charted their future course in the best interest of their profession. Theirs was an organized effort underlining their concern for the future of Savannah and Georgia. The pilots were determined to play a constructive role in what the future had to offer. Based on its past successful commercial role, they knew the Savannah River could become the strongest lifeline in the recovery of the state's economy after the war.

The pilots were soon proved right in their thinking. In 1865, the reconstruction era was launched by the people of Georgia, supported by state leadership. Deepening of the Savannah River was begun, first with city funds and later with federal assistance provided by the U.S. Army Corps of Engineers. In 1889, work was completed that took the channel to a depth of 20 feet, allowing ever-larger vessels to call on Savannah's port.

On December 15, 1895, under the Code of the State of Georgia, the corporate authorities for Savannah and nearby cities Darien, Brunswick, and St. Mary's were established, empowering each to appoint commissioners of pilotage. There were seven commissioners whose terms were appointed to be one, two, three, four, five, six, and seven years respectively. Under the law, commissioners were given authority to appoint pilots who had to be "U.S. citizens of good character, and most fit to act as pilots." In addition, the pilots were to be licensed and be skilled in navigation or exporters engaged in active business at the respective ports.

Under the law each port was assigned a specific number of pilots: 20 for the port of Savannah, 15 for the port of Brunswick, 10 for the port of Darien, 8 for the port of St. Mary's and 4 pilots for the great Satilla River. The law further stated that only licensed pilots could receive a fee or gratuity for conducting or piloting any vessel inward or outward from any of the ports, rivers or harbors for which a pilot was licensed. Anyone piloting vessels without a pilot's license or having a suspended or revoked license would be guilty of violating the law.

Commissioners had the authority to prescribe rules and regulations for the governance of pilots and to also set the fees for their services. They were given the authority to suspend or revoke a pilot's license for lack of skill, fitness, negligence, or carelessness.

Since the association's founding, the commissioners and members of the Savannah Pilots Association have seen and experienced changes in both the Savannah River itself and the nature of commerce in general. The river channel was gradually deepened from 10 feet to its present depth of 42 feet. Many bridges were removed or replaced, including the Talmadge Bridge, which was torn down and re-created with a beautiful, modern 185-foot span for vertical clearance.

At the same time, world events such as the Industrial Revolution, the Great Depression, the Energy Crisis of the early 1970s, the events of September 11, 2001 and multiple economic downturns and recessions -not to mention numerous wars and conflicts- impacted how business was conducted. But during all these changes, one thing has remained constant: the professionalism of the pilots themselves. Their superior skills and commitment to "Safety First" have enabled them to perform above their own standards for all these years.

Today, the members of the Savannah Pilots Association continue to do what they have always done - safely guide the vessels in their charge in and out of the ports they serve. It has been a remarkable 142 years and Savannah's future only looks brighter. To that end, the pilots will always play a significant role in the city's success.

Colonial Group, Inc.

When Raymond M. Deméré founded the corporation that would
become the Colonial Group, Inc. in the early 1920's,
he had little more than his imagination to go on.

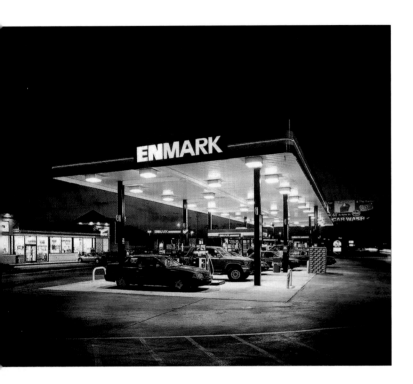

Over the decades, the company has grown steadily, expanding into new markets throughout the South and cultivating business relationships that span the globe.

Colonial Oil Industries, Enmark Stations, and Colonial Terminals have shown steady growth. The company has expanded into other industries that include tug and barge services, natural gas marketing, blue water marine services, chemical distribution, kaolin storage and handling as well as a motor fuels operation in Puerto Rico.

However, as the facilities and operations have become decidedly more modern, the corporate philosophy has remained the same - to be successful you must always earn the respect and confidence of those with whom you do business. That belief is not only the cornerstone of Colonial Oil's successful past, but also the foundation of its bright future.

From a barrel of oil to a bundle of industries, the story of the Colonial Group has been marked by impressive accomplishments and an unwavering dedication to the vision of the man who started it all. In following Raymond Deméré's example of hard work and the commitment to customers, the Colonial Group has furthered his greatest legacy - success.

He had just returned home to Savannah, Georgia, in 1921 after serving in World War I and decided to go into business for himself. Given America's newfound fascination with the "gasoline buggy," whose engines were fueled by petroleum products, the business he chose was one of great promise.

Armed with only one barrel of lubricating oil, he founded "American Oil Company," which began with just a warehouse, but soon added storage tanks, and later, company-owned filling stations around the Savannah area.

In 1933, the company became known as "Colonial Oil," and even greater expansion began. Envisioning opportunities for the distribution of petroleum products at Savannah's port, Deméré began construction on an independent ocean terminal and storage facility. It soon became the largest of its kind in the Southeast, and today the facility occupies more than 100 acres of prime Savannah River frontage.

Upon the death of Raymond Deméré in 1953, Charles L. Jarrell became president and then chairman, serving with the company until 1958. Thereafter, the leadership fell into the hands of Robert H. Deméré, the founder's son, who formed a retail subsidiary in 1963. Originally called "Interstate Stations," this unit later became known as Enmark Stations and now spans Georgia and the Carolinas.

Robert Deméré later became chairman in 1986, succeeded as president by his son, Robert H. Deméré, Jr.

STAR HARDANGER
BERGEN

Index